I0796561

This book is dedicated to
Ju's mother, with deepest love,
gratitude and remembrance.

MADELEINES

HYOJU PARK RONG YAO SOH
OF MADELEINE DE PROUST PÂTISSERIE

1 PERFECT MADELEINES STEP BY STEP

2 TRADITIONAL CLASSICS

3 CHILDHOOD COMFORT

6 FRUITY & VIBRANT

7 INDULGENT

4
ASIAN INSPIRED

5
DIETARY FRIENDLY

8
SEASONAL & CELEBRATION

9
SAVOURY

WHAT IS A MADELEINE?

A madeleine is a small French pastry, instantly recognisable by its delicate shell shape. It's golden at the edges, soft and buttery inside, and best enjoyed warm with tea or coffee. There's a quiet simplicity to a madeleine – unassuming, but always special.

At Madeleine de Proust, we use the madeleine as our canvas. We play with flavours, textures and fillings, giving this humble pastry a new story in every bite. For us, each madeleine isn't just a treat – it's a way to surprise, comfort and connect. Whether it's classic or something wildly inventive, every madeleine we create is a chance to share a little joy.

MADE IN KOREA
woojung

OUR MADELEINE DE PROUST

The phrase 'madeleine de Proust' comes from a famous scene in Marcel Proust's novel, *À la recherche du temps perdu* (In Search of Lost Time). In it, the main character dips a madeleine into his tea, and with one bite, childhood memories come flooding back – intense, vivid and completely unexpected. You might know a similar moment from the film *Ratatouille*, when Anton Ego tastes a dish and is instantly transported to his mother's kitchen. It's a powerful reminder: taste can hold memories, and something small can reconnect us to a forgotten feeling or place.

Rong and I met in 2016 when we were both studying Culinary Arts and Management at the University of West London. I'm from Korea, Rong is from Malaysia. We started as classmates, and soon became a couple, sharing not only our studies but our dreams for the future. After graduation, we went our separate ways for a while – different kitchens, different cities – but we always stayed close.

A few years later, our paths crossed again in Melbourne. I had just left my job at Attica, and Rong raised a question we'd talked about many times before: 'Do you still want to do something together?' This time, it felt right.

At first, we imagined opening a choux pastry shop – a single-product concept, something focused and fun. But as we brainstormed flavours and names, one stood out: Madeleine de Proust.

We had never heard the phrase before, but something about it felt special. We looked it up and discovered its meaning in French: a taste or scent that brings back an old memory. Something small, but deeply evocative. It was beautiful – quiet, but deep. The name lingered, and it made us wonder: should we do madeleines instead?

Suddenly, it all started to connect for me. When I was twelve, I loved watching K-dramas – especially *My Name is Kim Sam Soon*. There's a scene where the main character explains how to eat a madeleine the 'Proust way' – slowly, gently dipped into tea. She even calls it a 'sexy cookie' because of the hump. I didn't understand the meaning then, but writing this book made me realise that scene planted a seed: the idea that pastry could be beautiful and expressive. Maybe that's when I first dreamed of becoming a pastry chef.

Two years later, when I was fourteen, I made my first madeleine in an after-school baking class. I didn't know anything about technique, but I remember the smell of butter and how golden the shell looked. I was so proud to bring them home.

Years later, when Rong and I started planning the shop, that memory came back to me – like something had come full circle. Perhaps this is my madeleine de Proust: the place where everything started.

So we followed that feeling. And here we are.

MADELEINE
DE PROUST

MADELEIN
MADELEIN

IN THE SHAPE OF MEMORY

Rong arrived in Melbourne in February 2020 – just one month before the COVID lockdown. He had barely started at Matilda 159 when suddenly he was told the restaurant wouldn't need him until further notice. Like so many others during that strange time, he found himself at home, with no kitchen to work in and plenty of time to spare. He began baking, seriously exploring pastry for the first time.

One of the moulds he'd bought was a beautiful Chiyoda madeleine tray from Japan. The first time we baked with it, we instantly fell in love. The smell, the texture, the taste and that exact moment when the tray came out of the oven – it was simple but unforgettable. The madeleines tasted as if butter and a cloud had a baby – golden, fluffy, melt-in-your-mouth soft. That moment stayed with us.

But soon life resumed. Lockdown ended and we both returned to busy restaurant kitchens. After four years at Attica, I left my role as head pastry chef and, finally, we decided it was time to give our own idea a go.

We ordered a few professional-grade moulds from Japan – the kind that only fit into a baker's oven (60 × 40cm/24 × 26in) and started looking for a commercial kitchen to rent. Nothing seemed to fit. Some kitchens had the right oven but were too far away. Some were close but couldn't fit our trays. The search was frustrating and exhausting.

In the end, we rented two kitchens: one in Footscray, where we did all the baking and finishing and another in Collingwood, where we prepped batter and decorations and set up our pick-up point. It was chaotic, but somehow we made it work.

For our first-ever pop-up, we ambitiously decided to offer eight different flavours, each requiring its own unique batter. Most bakeries wisely use a single batter with different fillings, but, of course, we chose the hard way.

We had 96 pre-orders, each box containing eight madeleines, meaning nearly 800 pieces to bake. We started baking at 2pm the day before and didn't finish until 6am the next morning. The moment we woke up, Rong called his mum and brother to help with the packing. Pick-up was at 9am. We had exactly three hours to pack everything and deliver it to Worksmith in Collingwood.

We were exhausted. I remember looking at each other and laughing: how did we end up here? Then customers started arriving, picking up boxes of our madeleines. That feeling is something we'll never forget. It was joy, disbelief and pride all at once. We had created something and people came.

After the pick-up, Rong jumped into the car and made deliveries across Melbourne in every direction. We had no planned route, no system, just boxes and tired eyes. We finally got home around 4pm, showered and immediately passed out. We didn't wake up until the next afternoon.

We had many days like that. Sometimes we forgot ingredients at the other kitchen and Rong had to drive back and forth across town. Other times, we worked so quickly and intensely that we'd almost fall asleep standing up. But looking back, those moments remain some of our most cherished memories. It wasn't perfect, but it was completely ours.

After a few months, we began looking for a permanent space and that became our little shop on Lygon Street.

Along the way, we met so many kind people who helped shape Madeleine de Proust into what it is today and without whom our dream would never have become reality. And our customer base grew and grew.

People have shared with us their happiness and their sadness – birthdays, breakups, new babies, farewells, quiet Sunday mornings. One story especially touches our hearts: a couple first tried our madeleines on their wedding anniversary, and they've returned every year since. It became their tradition and, somehow, we became part of it. We never imagined our little pastries could mean so much, but we're truly grateful to be part of these moments.

Madeleine de Proust wasn't just born from a recipe. It came from tired hands, late nights, burnt trays, surprise joy – and above all, a lot of heart.

BANANA
BANANA
BANANA
BANANA
BANANA
BANANA

MADELEINE
DE PROUST

This isn't a strict manual or a rule book. It's a collection of everything we've learned after baking madeleines again and again. We made mistakes, fixed them and kept on striving for perfection. To begin your journey, you will get the best results if you follow the guidance and techniques carefully. Once you have mastered the basics, you can start experimenting. Some of the recipes are simple and familiar, some are a little more technical, but you will learn something from each one – as we did – because each recipe teaches something.

PERFECT MADELEINES STEP BY STEP

HOW TO USE THIS BOOK

Please read through this first section before you start baking – it may save you a few surprises and will make your experience smoother. We include details from greasing the mould and mixing the batter to glazing and finishing your madeleines. You'll notice some recipes have a 'Keep It Simple' section for a straightforward bake, plus an extra 'Feeling Confident?' step for when you want to take it further. The 'Feeling Confident?' version might include extra steps like chocolate tempering or chocolate dipping, which you can skip if you're baking at home for the first time. The short or simple version lets you enjoy the full flavour of the madeleine without the extra hassle.

You'll also find a few basic recipes, grouped after the main recipe pages, so feel free to refer back to them when needed.

INGREDIENTS

We have included a whole range of exciting flavours but we chose ingredients you can actually find, because baking shouldn't feel impossible. It should feel possible, even a little exciting.

MEASURING

You may find this slightly different from other cookbooks because we measure all our ingredients in grams. That's the way all bakers and pastry chefs work because it is the most accurate. You'll soon get used to it. For this book, we had already adjusted the recipe to suit everyone.

MOULDS

Each recipe specifies the mould we used and there's lots of information on the options on page 25. But please, don't stop just because you don't have the same moulds as us. Any mould is okay.

The shape of the madeleines might look different, but the flavour and the feeling will still be beautiful. You can use a muffin tray, a round silicone mould, even a small baking pan if you like. Use our recipes as a guide, but trust yourself too. Create your own version. Make it yours.

OVENS

The methods in this book are written for a convection or fan oven at home, but we have included the temperature for standard ovens, too. You'll also find more baking information on page 34.

BUILD YOUR OWN MADELEINE

These are the main elements to creating your madeleines:

MOULD SHAPE Classic shell, mini, round or anything you like.
BASE FLAVOUR Citrus, nutty, floral, chocolate or something you love.
FILLING (OPTIONAL) Custard, ganache, buttercream or jam.
GLAZE (OPTIONAL) Chocolate or fruit-based.
COATING (OPTIONAL) Nuts, crumbs, chocolate shell or marshmallow.
DECORATION (OPTIONAL) Flowers, gold leaf or sprinkles.

Our madeleines come from memories. From places we've lived. From things we've tasted and little ideas we mixed together. We hope you do the same.

Try to open your mind. Use what's inside this book to find your own style, your own madeleine.

This book is for anyone who is curious and wants to create. With butter, sugar and a little bit of imagination, you can create your unique madeleine de Proust!

INGREDIENTS

Before you start baking, it helps to get to know your ingredients. With madeleines, even the simplest components – like butter, eggs and flour make a big difference in taste and texture. We recommend using the best ingredients you can find (and afford). In this section, you'll find some notes on the key ingredients we use most often, along with tips for choosing or substituting them at home.

BAKING POWDER

We use baking powder, not bicarbonate of soda (baking soda). It activates twice: once when mixed and again in the oven, giving madeleines their signature hump.

BUTTER

Use unsalted butter with at least 83% fat content. We like to use a blend of butter from France, Australia and New Zealand to balance depth of flavour and aroma.

Cultured butter has more complexity but its acidity may impact rise and texture. If using it, be ready to adjust your recipe (resting time, temperature or baking powder) for best results.

For dairy-free recipes, we use a plant-based alternative and recommend choosing one that's high in fat, with minimal added water or emulsifiers. Avoid strongly flavoured or infused varieties, as they can easily overpower delicate ingredients. We use Nuttelex.

CHOCOLATE

Quality chocolate is essential, so look for high-quality couverture chocolate (not compound chocolate) with at least 70% cocoa solids, or as specified in the recipe. Compound chocolate usually contains vegetable fats (like palm or coconut oil) instead of cocoa butter. Couverture will specify cocoa butter as the main fat and often mentions 'couverture' on the label.

We mainly use Valrhona and Republica del Cacao couverture chocolates in this book for their smooth melt, flavour consistency and ideal cocoa-butter content. They're excellent for both fillings and coatings.

Another chocolate we like to use is caramelized white chocolate, known as Dulcey – inspired by dulce de leche – from Valrhona.

COCOA POWDER

In some recipes we use Dutch-processed cocoa powder for its deep colour and smooth, mellow flavour. Dutch-processed cocoa is alkalized, which reduces acidity and creates a richer taste. If you can't find Dutch-processed cocoa powder, regular unsweetened cocoa powder works as well.

EGGS

We always use free-range eggs, weighed without shells for accuracy.

After cracking, we gently blend the eggs using a hand blender (not a whisk), then strain them to remove the chalazae (the protein that holds the yolk in the egg). This creates a smoother, more uniform batter.

Note that egg quality varies with seasons. Warmer months (when hens drink more water) lead to thinner whites and paler yolks, which can subtly affect the structure and rise of your madeleines.

FLOUR

We use cake flour in all our recipes. Cake flour – sometimes called sponge flour or soft flour – has a lower protein content than plain (all-purpose) flour, usually around 7 – 9%. The lower the protein, the softer and more delicate the crumb.

In our kitchen, we use Nisshin Violet, a premium Japanese cake flour with 7.8% protein and a superfine texture. It's not just any flour; it's a key ingredient that makes our madeleines truly unique. Nisshin Violet's low-gluten potential is what gives our madeleines their signature soft crumb and crispy outer layer.

If you can't find Nisshin Violet, try to source the lowest-protein cake flour you can. For the closest result, replace 10% of your cake flour with cornflour (cornstarch).

HONEY

Honey adds flavour, colour and moisture. It's also hygroscopic, helping to keep madeleines tender. We select honey based on the recipe:

HONEY FROM LOCAL PRODUCERS We like to use honey produced locally, since Australia has so many excellent small producers and farmers. Raw and unfiltered honey gives a bright, clean flavour.

LEATHERWOOD A special honey, which is bold, floral and slightly wild.

SUGAR

We use several kinds of sugar but mainly caster (superfine) sugar.

CASTER SUGAR This dissolves quickly and evenly, making it ideal for batter structure and caramelization.

ICING (CONFECTIONERS') SUGAR We use this for glazes, to give a smooth, glossy finish.

GLUCOSE SYRUP This adds stability and elasticity, especially in fillings. It has about 30 – 50% the sweetness of regular sugar.

INVERTED SUGAR This helps retain moisture, prevent crystallization and improve mouthfeel in ganache or glaze. Its sweetness is about 120 – 130% that of regular sugar. We generally use Trimoline.

EQUIPMENT

You don't need a professional kitchen to make beautiful madeleines at home, but having the right tools does make things easier (and a little more fun). Here's a quick rundown of the equipment we use most often, plus a few suggestions for helpful extras. If you're missing something, don't worry – there are usually ways to improvise!

MOULDS

Choosing the right mould isn't just about aesthetics; it directly affects how your madeleines bake. The material, depth and coating can influence rise, texture, shell definition and crust.

For all the recipes in this book, we primarily use a 22mm (⅝in) deep mould from either Woojung or Chiyoda Both perform exceptionally well. Woojung is more accessible internationally and offers great value, so we recommend it if you want to replicate the results in this book.

POPULAR MOULD TYPES

KOREAN (WOOJUNG)
MATERIAL Carbon steel with SILPAP non-stick coating.
PERFORMANCE Deep wells create full-bodied madeleines with strong rise and golden crust.
BEST FOR Professionals and serious home bakers.

JAPANESE (CHIYODA)
MATERIAL Tin-plated steel with silicone coating.
PERFORMANCE Heats evenly, releases cleanly without greasing and produces sharp shell definition.
BEST FOR Professionals and serious home bakers.

FRENCH (GOBEL, MATFER, DE BUYER)
MATERIAL Tin-plated or coated steel.
PERFORMANCE Crisp crust and elegant form, especially when well-buttered and floured.
BEST FOR Lovers of traditional French-style madeleines.

STANDARD NON-STICK METAL (E.G. USA PAN, CHICAGO METALLIC)
MATERIAL Aluminized or carbon steel with non-stick coating.
PERFORMANCE Reliable for beginners; decent crust but slightly softer definition.
BEST FOR Everyday use or entry-level bakers.

SILICONE
MATERIAL Food-grade silicone, sometimes reinforced with fibreglass.
PERFORMANCE Easiest to unmould, but produces pale, soft madeleines with minimal hump.
BEST FOR Beginner-friendly or dessert-style madeleines.

TIP

Even high-end moulds like Woojung or Chiyoda may eventually start sticking as their coatings wear. In that case, lightly butter and flour the moulds before use (page 29).

OTHER ESSENTIAL TOOLS

APPLE CORER
To make a neat cavity for fillings.

BAKING PARCHMENT
Keeps trays clean and protects against glaze drips.

BLOW TORCH
For torching meringue or sugar crusts.

CHOCOLATE SETTING RACK
This is useful when you are coating madeleines.

COOLING RACK OR PERFORATED TRAY
Helps avoid soggy bases and promotes even crusts.

DIGITAL SCALE
For precision. Always weigh ingredients.

HAND BLENDER
Ideal for emulsifying ganache or curds.

MIXING BOWLS
Metal or glass for folding and heating; use polypropylene or glass for chocolate tempering.

PASTRY BRUSH
A soft-bristle brush works for greasing or glazing.

PIPING BAG
For clean and consistent portioning.

SIEVE
For sifting flour or straining egg mixtures.

SPATULA
For folding and scraping.

STAND MIXER
Useful for meringue, buttercream or larger batches of batter.

THERMOMETER
For monitoring butter, chocolate and egg temperatures.

WHISK
For mixing wet ingredients and forming emulsions.

ZESTER
For finely zesting citrus.

Astro

Microplane

HOW TO PREPARE YOUR MOULD

The traditional madeleine is made in the classic shell-shaped moulds but there are all sorts of shapes and sizes you can experiment with, from teddy bears, mini-cakes and bananas to cats, crowns and cacao pods. We have listed the mould we have used for each individual recipe but you can choose whatever you prefer. Whatever the size of your mould, you want to fill the cavities 80% full, so if you choose a smaller mould than the one specified, stick to the 80%-full rule. You can make more madeleines and bake for a shorter time.

A properly prepared mould ensures clean release, defined shape and a beautifully even crust. Different materials require different approaches. Here's how we prepare ours.

STEEL MOULDS

If you're using Chiyoda or Woojung moulds and they're still in good condition, you can usually skip the butter-and-flour step. Simply wipe a very thin layer of neutral oil (like grapeseed) over each cavity using a soft tissue.

BUTTER-AND-FLOUR METHOD

To protect the coating and extend the mould's life, you can also use this traditional butter-and-flour method.

- Use softened butter (not melted) and brush an even layer over each cavity.
- Dust lightly with strong flour or bread flour – the larger particles help with release.
- For chocolate-based recipes, use cocoa powder instead.
- Turn the coated mould upside down and tap gently to remove the excess.

SILICONE MOULDS

Spray the mould generously with oil spray. This helps improve colourization and surface definition.

Always place the silicone mould on a baking tray before filling and baking to ensure even heat distribution and support.

TIP

For a flatter hump – especially useful when building madeleine towers (page 127) – place a second mould of the same size gently on top during baking. This lightly compresses the rise and creates a more level surface. It works especially well with silicone moulds.

THE MIXING METHOD STEP BY STEP

Let's start with how you create the batter for your madeleines. While each recipe in this book has its own flavour and personality, the base method stays pretty consistent. Master this and you'll have the foundation to build madeleines of every kind.

1 PREP EVERYTHING FIRST

Mise en place is your best friend.

BUTTER

Melt gently over a bain-marie to 40°C (104°F). If your recipe includes milk or oil, warm them together.

EGGS

Crack the eggs into a heatproof bowl, lightly blend with a hand blender (just enough to combine), then strain through a sieve.

DRY INGREDIENTS (EXCLUDING SUGAR)

Sift your flour, baking powder, salt, tea powder, milk powder, spices or other powders. Set aside. (Sugar is added separately in the next step.)

2 WARM THE EGGS, SUGAR & HONEY

EGGS, CASTER SUGAR, HONEY AND ANY AROMATICS

Combine these ingredients in a separate bowl, including things like vanilla or citrus zest.

STIR GENTLY

Place the bowl over a bain-marie and stir gently with a whisk – don't whip, just help the sugar dissolve. Keep stirring until all the sugar dissolves and the mixture maintains a temperature of around 30°C (86°F). Use a thermometer.

GENTLE WARMING

This activates the lecithin (a natural emulsifier in egg yolks), which helps bind fat and liquid in the next steps. It also ensures a smoother batter and more even rise.

3 ADD THE DRY INGREDIENTS

MIX GENTLY BUT THOROUGHLY

Whisk the sifted dry ingredients into the warm egg mixture until fully smooth – no lumps, no streaks.

This stage is critical for structure. Take about 1 – 2 minutes to ensure it's well-combined, but avoid overmixing to prevent gluten development.

OVERMIXED BATTER GIVES A TOUGH CRUMB AND LESS HUMP

Mixing too much after adding the flour develops the gluten, which tightens the batter's structure. That will give you:

- Dense, less delicate crumb.
- A flat or uneven hump.
- Chewy texture.

4 EMULSIFY THE BUTTER

NOW BRING IN YOUR WARM MELTED BUTTER

It should still be at 40°C (104°F). Add it in three stages – pour in one-third, mix well, then repeat twice. This gradual incorporation creates a stable emulsion where fat is evenly dispersed through the batter.

The mixture should turn glossy, smooth and cohesive. A little extra mixing at the end helps lock it in, but keep it gentle.

BUTTER TEMPERATURE MATTERS

Butter must be added warm (40 – 45°C/104 – 113°F)) for proper emulsification:

- Too cold leads to streaks or separation.
- Too hot can destabilize the egg mixture or partially cook it.

5 PIPE & BAKE

TRANSFER TO YOUR PREPARED MOULD

Pour and spoon your batter into a piping bag, then fill each cavity about 80% full. For our standard 22mm (⅝in) Chiyoda or Woojung moulds, that's about 35g (1 ¼oz) per cavity.

Your batter is now ready to bake – no chilling required.

ALL ABOUT CHILLING

Here's why some recipes recommend chilling batter and why we don't.

Why some recipes chill:

- **THERMAL SHOCK** Cold batter hitting a hot oven causes rapid expansion → bigger hump.
- **BUTTER SOLIDIFICATION** Firmer batter structure helps maintain shape during early baking.
- **GLUTEN RELAXATION AND HYDRATION** Resting allows gluten to relax and flour to fully hydrate, giving a softer texture.

We've designed our batter to bake immediately, without compromising on rise or texture. It works because:

- **EMULSIFICATION** The batter is mixed at optimal temperature, ensuring full emulsification.
- **PRECISE FAT DISTRIBUTION** Our recipe carefully balances liquid, fat, and leavening to ensure even expansion during baking.
- **PROPERLY STRUCTURED BATTER** A well-developed emulsion traps air and water efficiently creating the structure needed for lift and a delicate crumb without requiring chilling to achieve it.

This means you still get a beautiful hump, delicate crumb and a crisp edge without the wait. Why wait, if you don't have to?

BAKING YOUR MADELEINES

Throughout the recipes, when you reach the baking step, refer back to this page to make sure your technique is correct and you get the best results. This stage is where everything comes together, the hump rises and the shell turns golden, but only if your oven is working with you, not against you.

CHOOSING THE RIGHT OVEN TEMPERATURE

Always preheat your oven before baking to ensure consistent internal heat and bake on the middle rack for the most even heat and consistent rise.

TIP

Use an oven thermometer to double-check your temperature, as many home ovens can be off by quite a bit!

FOR STEEL MOULDS

HOME OVEN (FAN / CONVECTION)
Preheat to 210°C fan (230°C/450°F/gas 9). Once the tray goes in, reduce to 180°C fan (400°F/gas 6) and bake for 10 – 12 minutes until the tops feel firm to the touch.

HOME OVEN (CONVENTIONAL / NO FAN)
Preheat to 240°C (428°F/gas maximum). Once the tray goes in, reduce to 180°C (350°F/gas 6) and bake for 10 – 12 minutes until the tops feel firm to the touch.

DECK OVEN
Preheat to 220°C (430°F/gas maximum). Once the tray goes in, reduce to 200°C (350°F/gas 6) and bake for 10 – 12 minutes until the tops feel firm to the touch.

COMBI OVEN
Preheat to 200°C fan (350°F/gas 6). Once the tray goes in, reduce to 180°C fan (400°F/gas 6) and bake until the tops feel firm to the touch.

FOR SILICONE MOULDS

These times and temperatures are for standard-sized madeleines (around 35g (1¼ oz) each). If using smaller moulds, reduce the baking time slightly.

HOME OVEN (FAN-FORCED / CONVECTION)
Preheat to 200°C (400°F). Once the tray goes in, reduce to 180°C (350°F) and bake for 10 – 12 minutes.

HOME OVEN (CONVENTIONAL / NO FAN)
Preheat to 220°C (425°F/gas 7). Once the tray goes in, reduce to 180°C (350°F/gas 6) and bake for 11 – 13 minutes.

DECK OVEN
Preheat to 200°C (410°F). Once the tray goes in, reduce to 180°C (350°F/gas 4) and bake for 11 – 13 minutes.

COMBI OVEN
Preheat to 205°C (405°F). Once the tray goes in, reduce to 180°C (350°F/gas 4) and bake for 11 – 13 minutes.

TEST AND ADJUST FOR YOUR OVEN

Every oven has its own 'personality'. If it's your first time baking madeleines with a new recipe or oven, we strongly recommend doing a small test batch of 2 – 3 madeleines first. Observe:

RISING How fast do they rise?

BROWNING Are they browning too quickly?

SETTING Are they setting properly?

Make small adjustments based on what you see.

TIP FOR BURSTING MADELEINES

If you're using a fan oven and your madeleines keep bursting or leaking, place a metal tray at the back to block some of the fan. This creates a gentler baking environment, similar to a deck oven.

AFTER BAKING

Once your madeleines are done:

UNMOULD Immediately remove them from the mould.

COOL Rest them on a perforated tray (like a baguette tray) or a wire rack to cool slightly. This prevents moisture build-up and keeps the shells crisp.

HOW TO FILL YOUR MADELEINES

Filling a madeleine transforms it from a humble sponge into something layered and full of character. Sometimes the filling is hidden as a surprise in the centre; other times, it becomes part of the decoration. No matter the style, the method is nearly always the same. Here's how we do it.

CHOOSE YOUR APPLE CORER

A thin, sharp apple corer works best – it gives you a clean, controlled cut without tearing the sponge.

DIG FROM THE FRONT OR THE HUMP

Twist the corer gently left and right as you press into the madeleine. You can enter from either the front face or the hump side, depending on the design. Stop at about 80% depth – don't go all the way through.

REMOVE THE CORE

Pull out the sponge plug carefully. If it doesn't come out all at once, you can always use a toothpick to dig out a bit more. Some recipes call for keeping it to reseal the madeleine later, while others don't require it.

FILL WITH CARE

Use a piping bag or a squeezy bottle (especially for jam or thinner fillings). Your filling should be soft enough to pipe easily but thick enough to hold its shape. If it's too runny, it'll sink or disappear into the sponge.

TOP-UP IF NEEDED

Jam and curd tend to sink slightly after a few minutes – they get absorbed by the crumb or settle into air pockets inside. After your first fill, wait 2 – 3 minutes, then top it up again so the surface sits flush.

REPLACE THE CORE (IF REQUIRED)

If the recipe calls for sealing the filling, trim the reserved core down to about 1cm (½in) and gently press it back into place. This gives a smooth finish and locks the filling inside.

HOW TO GLAZE YOUR MADELEINES

Glazing does more than just protect the madeleine from air and help it stay moist a little longer. It also adds a delicate sweetness and a thin, crisp texture to each bite, along with an extra layer of flavour. Here's how we glaze ours.

CLASSIC GLAZE

COOL Make sure your madeleines are completely cooled (about 30 minutes after baking) and filled (if needed). A cool, firm crust helps the glaze go on cleanly without picking up crumbs.

MIX If your glaze was made ahead, mix it well before using. You can warm it slightly in the microwave to loosen the texture, just enough to return it to a smooth, brushable consistency.

GET EVERYTHING READY Line a baking tray with baking parchment or a Teflon sheet. Wet your pastry brush with water. Wear gloves, if you like, for a cleaner grip.

BRUSH ON THE GLAZE Hold the madeleine in your non-dominant hand (e.g. left hand if you're right-handed). Brush the glaze onto the hump side first, then flip and glaze the front. Lay each glazed madeleine on its side on the prepared tray.

DRY To speed up drying, place the tray in a 130°C fan (300°F/gas 2) oven for 1 minute, then allow the madeleines to cool completely at room temperature.

CHOCOLATE ENROBAGE

This delightful French term simply means covering the madeleines in a thin layer of chocolate.

FREEZE YOUR MADELEINES: This works best if you are enrobing frozen cakes.

PREP YOUR EQUIPMENT: Prepare a chocolate-setting rack by covering a block of Styrofoam or a clean car sponge and putting it in a loaf pan or similar container. Skewer each frozen madeleine through the base.

MELT THE CHOCOLATE: Make sure your chocolate enrobage is fully emulsified and at the correct dipping temperature, typically 30 – 31°C (86 – 88°F).

COVER THE SKEWERS: Dip each madeleine fully into the chocolate, then lift it out and gently tap off the excess. Insert the skewer upright into the chocolate-setting rack and let the coating crystalize for a few minutes.

CHILL: Once partially set, transfer the skewered madeleines to the fridge to chill and finish setting.

FINISH: Carefully remove the skewers. Decorate however you like.

HOW TO TEMPER CHOCOLATE

For the home kitchen, we recommend the 'seeding method'. It's simple, reliable, and works well for most madeleine coatings and decorations. Here's how we do it.

Melt two-thirds of the chocolate over a pan of simmering water or in the microwave.

DARK CHOCOLATE: 50 – 55°C (120 – 130°F).
MILK, WHITE, BLONDE: 45 – 50°C (115 – 120°F).
VALRHONA INSPIRATION SERIES: 40 – 45°C (105 – 115°F).

Finely chop the remaining chocolate and add it little by little into the melted chocolate. Stir gently and continuously to cool it down to the desired temperature.

DARK CHOCOLATE: 28 – 29°C (82 – 84°F).
MILK CHOCOLATE: 27 – 28°C (81 – 82°F).
WHITE, BLONDE: 26 – 27°C (79 – 80°F).
VALRHONA INSPIRATION SERIES: 27 – 28°C (81 – 82°F).

Bring it back to working temperature, stirring gently:

DARK CHOCOLATE: 31°C (88°F).
MILK CHOCOLATE: 30°C (86°F).
WHITE, BLONDE: 29°C (84°F).
VALRHONA INSPIRATION SERIES: 30 – 31°C (86 – 88°F).

TEST BEFORE USING: Dip a knife or the back of a spoon into the chocolate, then place it in the fridge for 1 minute. If it sets with no streaks and a slight shine, it's ready.

Keep it in temper by gently warming with a heat gun or hair-dryer, if needed, but do not exceed 32°C (90°F). If the temperature goes above this, you will need to temper the chocolate again.

MADE IN KOREA
woojung

STORING AND REHEATING YOUR MADELEINES

Madeleines are generally best served on the day they are made but proper storage is key to keeping them at their best.

CLASSIC MADELEINES (GLAZED OR PLAIN)

ROOM TEMPERATURE: Store in an airtight container for up to 3 days.

FREEZING: For longer storage, freeze madeleines in an airtight container for up to 1 month.

TEXTURE AFTER 24 HOURS: After about 24 hours in an airtight container, madeleines naturally change. The crumb becomes a little more moist, the flavour deepens and the texture feels softer and richer. It's different from the fresh-out-of-the-oven feeling – less crisp at the edges, but rounder and more buttery inside. Some people even prefer them this way.

MADELEINES WITH FILLING

These are best enjoyed on the day they are made.

FREEZING: You can freeze madeleines with fillings such as ganache or jam, but not custard-based fillings. Fillings like custards or creams will affect the texture and freshness over time.

Could we stretch the shelf life? Technically, yes – by controlling water activity, moisture migration and other food-science factors. But honestly, it would take away from what makes a madeleine so special: its fresh, delicate texture and melt-in-your-mouth crumb.

REHEATING AND THAWING GUIDE

PLAIN WITHOUT GLAZE: Thaw uncovered at room temperature for 30 minutes, then reheat in the oven at 180°C fan (400°F/gas 6) for 2 minutes.

GLAZED OR FILLED: Thaw uncovered at room temperature for 30 minutes. No reheating needed.

TIP ON THAWING

Always thaw uncovered. Covering the madeleines while thawing can cause condensation, leading to sticky surface instead of a light, fresh finish.

BASIC RECIPES

SWISS BUTTERCREAM

INGREDIENTS

SWISS MERINGUE BASE
Egg whites 45g (1½oz)
Caster sugar 64.5g (2¼oz)
Salt ¼ tsp
Room temperature softened unsalted butter 150g (5¼oz)

METHOD

In a heatproof bowl, combine the egg whites, sugar and salt.

Set the bowl over a bain-marie and whisk gently until the mixture reaches 60°C (140°F).

Transfer to a stand mixer and whisk on high speed until stiff peaks form and the meringue is glossy and cool.

Reduce to medium speed and gradually add the softened butter in three additions. Continue whisking until the butter is fully incorporated and the buttercream is smooth and fluffy.

CARAMELISED MILK POWDER

MAKES

Yield varies depending on batch size

INGREDIENTS

Full cream milk powder – as needed

METHOD

STOVETOP METHOD

Place the milk powder in a stainless steel pan over medium heat.

Stir continuously with a heatproof spatula to prevent burning.

Toast until the powder turns a deep golden brown colour.

Transfer to a bowl and let cool completely before storing.

OVEN METHOD

Preheat the oven to 180°C (350°F/gas 4).

Spread the milk powder in a thin, even layer on a baking tray (do not overcrowd).

Bake for 5 minutes, then stir the powder well.

Continue toasting in 3 – 5 minute intervals, stirring between each, until they are all evenly golden brown.

Cool completely and store in an airtight container.

NUT PASTES

METHOD

HAZELNUTS

Roast at 160°C (320°F/gas 3) for 12 – 15 minutes, or until the skins crack and the nuts are golden and fragrant. Rub off the skins while still warm with a clean tea towel for a cleaner, sweeter flavor.

PISTACHIOS

Roast at 150°C (300°F/gas 2) for 8 – 10 minutes. Pistachios are more delicate – roast until just fragrant and lightly golden, but don't let them darken too much or they'll lose their fresh, green notes.

Once roasted and cooled, blend the nuts into a fine, smooth paste. Store in an airtight jar until ready to use.

MADELEINE

The classics are my go-to whenever I need a little comfort. There's something about their simple, familiar flavour, the golden edges, the soft crumb, the gentle sweetness that makes any moment feel a bit brighter. Whether you're sharing them with friends or just having one with your morning coffee, these madeleines have a way of fitting right in. They remind me that the best things in life are often the ones we reach for again and again, never getting old.

TRADITIONAL CLASSICS

BROWN BUTTER MADELEINES

MAKES

12

MOULD

Woojung / Chiyoda Madeleine
22mm (5⁄8 in) deep

This is where it all began. Our first madeleine took many tries to get just right – light, fluffy and consistent, like a cross between cake and cloud. We pair it with Tasmanian Leatherwood honey for a gentle floral lift that balances the richness. Instead of classic brown butter, we toast milk powder until deep golden to mimic those nutty, caramelized notes. This keeps the batter consistent and helps create that perfect hump every time. Be sure to revisit the full preparation instructions until the process feels natural.

INGREDIENTS

125g (4½oz) cake flour
5g (1 tsp) baking powder
3g (1 tsp) caramelized milk powder (page 47)
pinch of sea salt
105g (3½oz) butter
7g (1¼oz) milk
85g (3oz) whole eggs, strained (page 31)
80g (2¾oz) caster (superfine) sugar
10g (⅓oz) Leatherwood honey

METHOD

Preheat the oven to 210°C fan (450°F/gas 9) and prepare your mould (page 29).

Sift the flour, baking powder, caramelized milk powder and salt into a heatproof bowl, then set aside.

Melt the butter and milk together in a heatproof bowl over a pan of simmering water, keeping the temperature at 40°C (104°F).

Warm the eggs, sugar and honey to 30°C (86°F).

Mix the dry ingredients gently into the egg mixture, then mix in the butter one-third at a time.

Pipe into the moulds, reduce the oven temperature to 180°C (350°F/gas 4) and bake for 10 – 13 minutes until risen and set.

Unmould and leave to cool.

CHOCOLATE MADELEINES

MAKES

8

MOULD

Chiyoda cacao pod

Everyone has a chocolate treat that takes them back. Whether it's sneaking pieces from the pantry or sharing sweets with friends, chocolate has a way of making memories. This madeleine is rich in cocoa, with a gentle balance of softness and just a touch of grown-up depth.

INGREDIENTS

SIMPLE SYRUP

25g (¾oz) caster (superfine) sugar
25g (¾oz) water

CHOCOLATE MADELEINE BATTER

98g (3½oz) cake flour
10g (½oz) cocoa powder
3g (⅛oz) baking powder
pinch of sea salt
68g (2½oz) unsalted butter
4g (⅛oz) milk
55g (2oz) whole eggs, strained (see page 31)
52g (1¾oz) caster (superfine) sugar
7g (¼oz) honey

CHOCOLATE GLAZE

85g (3oz) icing (confectioners') sugar
7g (¼oz) cocoa powder
25g (¾oz) water

FOR DECORATION

edible gold powder

METHOD

SIMPLE SYRUP Combine the sugar and water in a small pan. Bring to the boil, then remove from heat and leave to cool.

CHOCOLATE MADELEINES Preheat the oven to 210°C fan (450°F/gas 9) and prepare your mould (page 29).

Sift together the flour, cocoa powder, baking powder and salt. Set aside.

In a heatproof bowl, melt the butter and milk together over a pan of simmering water, keeping the temperature at 40°C (104°F).

Warm the eggs, sugar and honey to 30°C (86°F).

Mix the dry ingredients gently into the egg mixture, then mix in the butter one-third at a time.

Pipe into the moulds, reduce the oven temperature to 180°C (350°F/gas 4) and bake for 10 – 13 minutes until risen and set.

Once baked, brush the madeleines with simple syrup while still warm.

CHOCOLATE GLAZE Sift the icing sugar and cocoa powder together into a bowl. Add the water and whisk until smooth. Use immediately or press clingfilm (plastic wrap) onto the surface to prevent drying out.

TO FINISH Once the madeleines are fully cooled, brush a thin layer of glaze over the surface (page 41). Allow to set at room temperature before serving. Add gold powder, if using.

VAL

YUZU MADELEINES

MAKES

12

MOULD

Woojung / Chiyoda Madeleine
22mm (⅝ in) deep

Yuzu – or yuja, as we call it in Korea – is one of my favourite citrus notes, floral, fresh, and full of brightness. My parents' hometown is known for yuja, and every winter we'd make yuja-cheong by mixing sliced yuja with sugar. This madeleine captures that same gentle tang and soft sweetness, bringing me right back to those winter days.

INGREDIENTS

YUZU SYRUP

25g (¾oz) caster (superfine) sugar
25g (¾oz) yuzu juice

LEMON MADELEINE BATTER

125g (4½oz) cake flour
5g (1 tsp) baking powder
pinch of sea salt
105g (3½oz) unsalted butter
7g (¼oz) milk
85g (3oz) whole eggs, strained (page 31)
80g (2¾oz) caster (superfine) sugar
10g (⅓oz) honey
4g grated lemon zest

YUZU GLAZE

80g icing (confectioners') sugar
20g yuzu juice

FINISH

grated yuzu or lemon zest

METHOD

YUZU SYRUP Combine the sugar and yuzu juice in a small pan. Bring to the boil, then remove from heat and leave to cool.

LEMON MADELEINE BATTER Preheat the oven to 210°C fan (450°F/gas 9) and prepare your mould (page 29).

Sift together the flour, baking powder and salt. Set aside.

In a heatproof bowl, melt the butter and milk over a pan of simmering water, keeping the temperature at 40°C (104°F).

Warm the eggs, sugar, honey and lemon zest to 30°C (86°F).

Mix the dry ingredients gently into the egg mixture, then mix in the butter one-third at a time.

Pipe into the moulds, reduce the oven temperature to 180°C (350°F/gas 4) and bake for 10 – 13 minutes until risen and set.

Once baked, brush each madeleine with yuzu syrup, while still warm.

YUZU GLAZE Sift the icing sugar and mix with yuzu juice until completely smooth.

TO FINISH Once the madeleines are completely cooled, brush a thin layer of yuzu glaze over each one. Zest some fresh yuzu or lemon over the top.

Let them air-dry at room temperature, or place in the oven at 130°C fan (300°F/gas 2) for 1 minute to speed up the drying process.

3

There's a special kind of comfort in these flavours. I didn't grow up with them, but I always wondered what they tasted like – soft bread, sweet jam, the warmth of cake fresh from the oven. Now I can capture those little wishes in every madeleine, and for a moment, it feels just like being a kid again...

CHILDHOOD COMFORT

CARROT CAKE MADELEINES

MAKES

12

MOULD

Woojung / Chiyoda Madeleine
22mm (⅝in) deep

I tasted my first carrot cake just after my induction day at university, in a little café called Farm W5 next to campus. Everything felt new – new country, new school, a sense of curiosity and adventure. Carrot cake had always seemed mysterious to me, but that first bite, spiced, soft and creamy, fit perfectly with the feeling of starting fresh. Now, whenever I make this, I'm reminded of that moment.

INGREDIENTS

CARAMELIZED CARROT

150g (5¼oz) carrot, grated
10–15g (2–2½tsp) grapeseed oil

CREAM CHEESE BUTTERCREAM

75g (2½oz) cream cheese
75g (2½oz) Swiss buttercream (page 46)
4g (scant tsp) grated lemon zest

CARROT CAKE MADELEINE BATTER

135g (4¾oz) cake flour
5g (1 tsp) baking powder
3g (¾ tsp) ground cinnamon
pinch of sea salt
115g (4oz) unsalted butter
7g (¼oz) milk
95g (3¼oz) whole eggs, strained (page 31)
85g (3oz) caster (superfine) sugar
10g (⅓oz) honey
65g (2¼oz) caramelized carrot (from above)
10g (⅓oz) toasted desiccated coconut

CINNAMON GLAZE

65g (2¼oz) icing (confectioners') sugar
15g (½oz) water
pinch of ground cinnamon

WALNUT CRUNCH

75g caramelized white chocolate or white chocolate
50g (1¾oz) toasted walnuts, roughly chopped
25g rice puffs, roughly crushed

FOR DECORATION (OPTIONAL)

edible rose gold powder

METHOD

Preheat the oven to 210°C fan (450°F/gas 9). Prepare your madeleine mould (page 29).

CARAMELIZED CARROT In a pan, cook the grated carrot with the grapeseed oil over medium heat for 10 minutes until lightly golden. Cool completely.

CREAM CHEESE BUTTERCREAM Soften the cream cheese in a stand mixer with a whisk attachment. Add Swiss buttercream and lemon zest, then whip until fluffy. Set aside in a piping bag.

CARROT CAKE MADELEINE BATTER Sift flour, baking powder, cinnamon and salt; set aside.

Melt butter and milk together in a heatproof bowl over simmering water, keeping temperature at 40°C (104°F).

Warm eggs, sugar and honey to 30°C (86°F).

Mix dry ingredients gently into the egg mixture, then mix in the butter one-third at a time. Fold in caramelized carrot and toasted coconut.

Pipe into the moulds, reduce the oven temperature to 180°C (350°F/gas 4) and bake for 10 – 13 minutes until risen and set.

Unmould and leave to cool.

CINNAMON GLAZE Mix icing sugar, water and cinnamon until smooth. Set aside.

AT THIS POINT, YOU CAN FINISH YOUR MADELEINES IN TWO WAYS:

KEEP IT SIMPLE

Core the back (hump side) of each cooled madeleine and fill with cream cheese buttercream, then close the lid. Glaze with cinnamon glaze and let dry.

FEELING CONFIDENT? TRY THIS:

WALNUT CRUNCH Melt chocolate to 40 – 45°C, add chopped walnuts and rice puffs, mix well and keep warm. If it hardens, simply microwave briefly.

TO FILL AND FINISH Core the front (shell side) of each cooled madeleine and fill with cream cheese buttercream. Freeze for 1 hour.

Spread the warm walnut rice crunch in the clean madeleine mould, and lightly press in the filled madeleine. Let set in the freezer for 30 minutes, covered lightly with cling film.

Unmould and brush with rose gold powder using a soft brush, if using.

MAKES

12

MOULD

Woojung / Chiyoda Madeleine
22mm (5/8in) deep

FRENCH TOAST MADELEINES

This madeleine first came about when we created our French-flavour theme box during our pick-up and delivery days. We wanted to capture the cosy comfort of French toast in one bite – soft and custardy inside, topped with a thin layer of brûlée crunch on the outside. The maple glaze melts into the crackly top, while a hint of cinnamon lingers in every bite. Sweet, golden and just a little bit crisp, it's a breakfast memory turned into dessert.

INGREDIENTS

VANILLA CUSTARD CREAM

100g (3¼oz) milk
30g (1oz) caster (superfine) sugar
½ teaspoon of vanilla paste
20g egg yolk
10g (⅓oz) cornflour (cornstarch)
10g (⅓oz) butter

MAPLE GLAZE

30g (1oz) icing (confectioners') sugar
25g (¾oz) hazelnut praline (optional)
10g (⅓oz) maple syrup, plus extra for finishing
pinch of ground cinnamon
10g (⅓oz) water

CINNAMON MADELEINE BATTER

125g (4½oz) cake flour
5g (1 tsp) baking powder
2g (½ tsp) ground cinnamon
pinch of sea salt
105g (3½oz) unsalted butter
7g (¼oz) milk
85g (3oz) whole eggs, strained (page 31)
80g (2¾oz) caster (superfine) sugar
10g (⅓oz) honey
3g (¾ tsp) grated orange zest
2g (⅓oz) ground cinnamon
pinch of fine salt

SUGAR COAT FOR THE BRÛLÉE

40g (2½oz) caster (superfine) sugar
pinch of fine salt

METHOD

Preheat the oven to 210°C fan (450°F/gas 9). Prepare your madeleine mould (page 29).

VANILLA CUSTARD CREAM Warm the milk, half of the sugar and the vanilla paste together in a pan.

In a separate bowl, whisk the egg yolk with the remaining sugar. Sift in the cornflour and mix well.

Gradually add the warm milk mixture into the egg mixture, whisking continuously.

Return the mixture to the pan and boil for 2 minutes, still whisking continuously.

Strain through a fine sieve, cover with clingfilm (plastic wrap) directly touching the surface and refrigerate until fully cooled.

Before use, whip with a paddle attachment or whisk until smooth.

MAPLE GLAZE Sift the icing sugar and whisk the rest of the ingredients together until smooth. Set aside.

CINNAMON MADELEINE BATTER Sift the flour, baking powder, cinnamon and salt then set aside.

Melt the butter and milk together in a heatproof bowl over a pan of simmering water, keeping the temperature at 40°C (104°F).

Warm the eggs, sugar, honey and orange zest to 30°C (86°F).

TO FILL Once the madeleines are completely cooled, dig out the core from the hump side and fill with vanilla custard cream. Close the filling by placing the removed core back.

AT THIS POINT, YOU CAN FINISH YOUR MADELEINES IN TWO WAYS:

KEEP IT SIMPLE Brush the madeleines thinly with maple glaze and let it air-dry.

Drizzle extra maple syrup over the top before serving.

FEELING CONFIDENT? TRY THIS:

TO MAKE THE SUGAR COAT FOR BRÛLÉE Mix the caster sugar and fine salt together. Set aside.

TO BRÛLÉE AND FINISH Brush a thin layer of water on the shell side and coat the front of the madeleine with the sugar mixture.

Brûlée with a blow torch until caramelized.

Finish by drizzling extra maple syrup over the top before serving.

S'MOREO MADELEINES

MAKES

12

MOULD

Woojung / Chiyoda Madeleine 22mm (⅝in) deep

Think of that first bite: a tender brown butter madeleine giving way to a creamy, cookie-studded Oreo ganache centre, then a fluffy layer of toasted marshmallow that pulls apart with a hint of gooey sweetness. The shell is crisp and sweet with white chocolate and crushed Oreo, cracking gently between your teeth. Each layer brings its own texture – nutty sponge, gooey marshmallow, creamy filling and a crunchy shell – all coming together in a nostalgic mashup. It's a little campfire s'more, a favourite Oreo snack, and the warmth of brown butter madeleines, all in one playful, chocolate-dipped treat.

INGREDIENTS

OREO GANACHE

100g (3¼oz) double (heavy) cream
40g (1½oz) caramelized white chocolate or white chocolate
35g (1¼oz) Oreo cookie (only the cookie part, not the icing), crushed by hand
pinch of sea salt

BROWN BUTTER MADELEINE BATTER

125g (4½oz) cake flour
5g (1 tsp) baking powder
3g (1 tsp) caramelized milk powder (page 47)
pinch of sea salt
105g (3½oz) butter
7g (¼oz) milk
85g (3oz) whole eggs, strained (page 31)
80g (2¾oz) caster (superfine) sugar
10g (⅓oz) honey

MARSHMALLOW

12g (¼oz) gelatine leaf
115g (4oz) caster (superfine) sugar
35g (1¼oz) water
50g (1¾oz) Trimoline A
37g (1¼oz) Trimoline B

OREO CHOCOLATE ENROBAGE

150g (5¼oz) white chocolate
35g (1¼oz) cocoa butter
15g (½oz) grapeseed oil
15g (½oz) Oreo cookies

METHOD

Preheat the oven to 210°C fan (450°F/gas 9). Prepare your madeleine mould.

OREO GANACHE Warm the cream in a pan to 80°C (175°F). Pour the hot cream over the white chocolate and blend with a hand blender. Fold in the hand-crushed Oreo cookies and sea salt.

Let crystallize overnight in the fridge.

BROWN BUTTER MADELEINE BATTER Sift together the flour, baking powder, caramelized milk powder and salt. Set aside.

In a heatproof bowl, melt the butter and milk over a pan of simmering water, keeping the temperature at 40°C (104°F).

Warm the eggs, sugar and honey to 30°C (86°F).

Mix the dry ingredients gently into the egg mixture, then mix in the butter one-third at a time.

Pipe into the moulds, reduce the oven temperature to 180°C (350°F/gas 4) and bake for 10 – 13 minutes until risen and set.

Remove from the oven, unmould and leave to cool.

TO FILL Once the madeleines are fully cooled, dig out the hump core and fill with Oreo ganache.

AT THIS POINT, YOU CAN FINISH YOUR MADELEINES IN TWO WAYS:

KEEP IT SIMPLE

Enjoy as is – a classic brown butter madeleine with an Oreo ganache centre.

FEELING CONFIDENT? TRY THIS:

MARSHMALLOW Soften the gelatine in iced water and place Trimoline B into the bowl of a stand mixer.

In a pan, heat the sugar, water and Trimoline A to 110°C (230°F). Add the softened gelatine and stir to dissolve completely. Pour the mixture into Trimoline B and whip on high speed until fluffy.

While whipping, use a blowtorch to lightly toast the marshmallow mixture for added flavour. Set aside at room temperature until ready to use.

OREO CHOCOLATE ENROBAGE Melt the white chocolate, cocoa butter and oil together to 35°C (95°F). Hand blend to emulsify well, then stir in the crushed Oreo cookies.

TO FINISH Dip the front of the filled madeleine into the marshmallow mixture. Press the dipped side gently into an oil-greased madeleine mould to hold its shape. Allow to set, then unmould carefully. (You can set it in the freezer to speed up the setting process, around 10 minutes.)

Insert a skewer into the base of each madeleine and freeze for at least 4 hours.

Dip each frozen madeleine into the Oreo chocolate enrobage. Tap off the excess and place upright in a chocolate-setting rack or lay flat on clingfilm (plastic wrap).

Let set in the freezer for 5 minutes, then remove the skewers.

Allow to come back to room temperature before serving.

MAKES

8

MOULD

Bread Toast Shaped

PEANUT BUTTER & JAM MADELEINES

I didn't grow up with peanut butter and jam sandwiches, but the idea always felt iconic – something you'd see in cartoons or tucked into lunchboxes on TV. When I moved to London and wandered supermarket aisles for the first time, I finally tried the real thing. The mix of creamy peanut butter and bright, tangy jam was instantly addictive. We wanted to play with that classic, so we baked madeleine batter in mini toast-shaped pans for a nostalgic twist. Soft and golden, each 'slice' is sandwiched with smooth peanut butter and a glossy layer of jam. Every bite is tender, a little salty, a little sweet, and completely comforting – like the childhood treat you always dreamed of, now with a baker's touch.

INGREDIENTS

STRAWBERRY JAM

100g (3¼oz) strawberry purée
50g (1¾oz) caster (superfine) sugar
50g (1¾oz) glucose syrup
5g (1 tsp) lemon juice

PEANUT BUTTER CREAM

100g (3¼oz) Swiss buttercream (page 46)
50g (1¾oz) smooth peanut butter

PEANUT BUTTER MADELEINE BATTER (20G PER MOULD)

93g (3¼oz) cake flour
3g (⅛oz) baking powder
small pinch of sea salt
62g (2¼oz) unsalted butter
23g (¾oz) peanut oil
23g (¾oz) smooth peanut butter
5g (1 tsp) milk
66g (2⅓oz) whole eggs, strained
62g (2¼oz) caster (superfine) sugar
7g (¼oz) honey

METHOD

STRAWBERRY JAM Combine the strawberry purée, sugar and glucose syrup in a pan. Boil over medium-high heat for 15 minutes, skimming off any foam that rises to the surface. Check consistency by dropping a small spoonful into cold water – if it holds its shape and doesn't spread, it's ready. Add lemon juice. Let cool completely.

PEANUT BUTTER CREAM Mix the buttercream and peanut butter together until fully incorporated. Keep aside.

PEANUT BUTTER MADELEINE Preheat the oven to 210°C fan (450°F/gas 9) and prepare your mould (page 29).

Sift together the flour, baking powder and salt. Set aside.

In a heatproof bowl, melt the butter, peanut oil, peanut butter and milk over a pan of simmering water, keeping the temperature at 40°C (104°F).

Warm the eggs, sugar and honey to 30°C (86°F).

Mix the dry ingredients gently into the egg mixture, then mix in the butter one-third at a time.

Pipe into the moulds, fill up to 15g or 40%, cover with baking paper and a flat tray, reduce the oven temperature to 180°C (350°F/gas 4) and bake for 10 – 13 minutes until the top is golden brown and flat.

Remove from the oven, unmould and leave to cool.

TO FINISH Once the madeleines are completely cooled, assemble them like a PB&J sandwich. Start by spreading a layer of the peanut butter cream and then spoon a dollop of strawberry jam and top with one more madeleine to finish off.

For us, these flavours aren't just inspirations, they're part of who we are. We grew up tasting, mugwort, pandan, matcha and black sesame in all kinds of ways, from street snacks to family favourites. Bringing them into madeleines feels like sharing a piece of our own story. Whenever I bake these, it's a gentle reminder of home.

ASIAN-
INSPIRED

MAKES

12

MOULD

Matsunaga Madeleine Bear

BLACK SESAME MADELEINES

Inspired by Dol Hareubang (Stone Grandpa) from Jeju, these madeleines are all about bold flavour and character. The black sesame brings deep, roasted nuttiness to the soft cake – intense and fragrant in every bite. The outside is playful and cute, while the taste inside is seriously rich. Sometimes we coat them in chocolate, sometimes we leave them plain, but either way, the flavour stands out.

INGREDIENTS

BLACK SESAME BUTTERCREAM

200g (7oz) Swiss buttercream (page 46)
15g (½oz) black sesame paste

BLACK SESAME GLAZE

65g (2¼oz) icing (confectioners') sugar
15g (½oz) water
5g (1 tsp) black sesame paste

BLACK SESAME MADELEINE BATTER

110g (3¾oz) cake flour
3g (¾ tsp) baking powder
pinch of sea salt
72g (2½oz) unsalted butter
25g (¾oz) black sesame paste
25g (¾oz) grapeseed oil
7g (¼oz) milk
80g (3oz) whole eggs, strained (page 31)
75g (2½oz) caster (superfine) sugar
10g (⅓oz) honey

BLACK SESAME CHOCOLATE SHELL

300g (10½oz) white chocolate
30g (1oz) black sesame paste

METHOD

BLACK SESAME BUTTERCREAM Whip the Swiss buttercream and black sesame paste together until fully incorporated. Set aside.

BLACK SESAME GLAZE Mix the icing sugar, water and black sesame paste until smooth. Set aside.

BLACK SESAME MADELEINE Preheat the oven to 210°C fan (450°F/gas 9) and prepare your mould (page 29).

Sift the flour, baking powder and salt into a bowl then set aside.

Melt the butter, black sesame paste, oil and milk together in a heatproof bowl over a pan of simmering water, keeping the temperature at 40°C (104°F).

Warm the eggs, sugar and honey to 30°C (86°F).

Mix the dry ingredients gently into the egg mixture, then mix in the butter one-third at a time.

Pipe into the moulds, reduce the oven temperature to 180°C (350°F/gas 4) and bake for 10 – 13 minutes until risen and set.

Remove from the oven, unmould and leave to cool. Spray lightly with syrup while still warm (optional).

AT THIS POINT, YOU CAN FINISH YOUR MADELEINES IN TWO WAYS:

KEEP IT SIMPLE

Glaze each cooled madeleine with black sesame glaze and leave to set (page 41).

Dig out the hump and fill with black sesame buttercream (page 38).

FEELING CONFIDENT? TRY THIS:

Glaze the hump side of each cooled madeleine with black sesame glaze and leave to dry.

TO ADD A CHOCOLATE SHELL:

Hand-blend the melted white chocolate and black sesame paste together, then temper. (page 42).

Pour 15g (½oz) into each mould cavity.

Gently press the glazed madeleine into the mould and let it set at room temperature for at least 4 hours (or set at room temp for 1 hour and keep in the fridge for 10 mins – check, as metal moulds in the fridge might cool down too fast and the chocolate shell might crack). Lightly cover the mould to prevent drying out.

Once fully set, carefully unmould.

MAKES

12

MOULD

Woojung / Chiyoda Madeleine
22mm (5⁄8in) deep

MATCHA RED BEAN MOCHI MADELEINES

We love matcha with red bean. We added mochi for an extra layer of chew – soft, stretchy and fun to pull apart. The earthy bitterness of matcha pairs perfectly with sweet, creamy red bean, while the mochi adds a gentle bounce to every bite. Best enjoyed fresh, while the mochi is still soft, tender and stretchable.

INGREDIENTS

MILK MOCHI FILLING

80g (2¾oz) glutinous rice flour
20g (¾oz) cornflour (cornstarch)
170g (6oz) milk
18g (5⁄8oz) caster (superfine) sugar
10g (3⁄8oz) butter

RED BEAN PASTE

(or purchase ready-made from an Asian supermarket)
100g (3½oz) red beans (adzuki beans)
500g water
50g (1¾oz) light soft brown sugar
5g (1 tsp) glucose syrup
pinch of sea salt

MATCHA MADELEINE BATTER

100g (3½oz) cake flour
10g (⅓oz) ceremonial matcha powder
5g (1 tsp) baking powder
pinch of sea salt
105g (3½oz) unsalted butter
7g (¼oz) milk
85g (3oz) whole eggs, strained (page 31)
75g (2½oz) caster (superfine) sugar
10g (⅓oz) honey

MATCHA GLAZE

78g (2¾oz) icing (confectioners') sugar
18g (5⁄8oz) water
4g (⅛oz) ceremonial matcha powder

FOR DECORATION

10g (⅓oz) ceremonial matcha powder, for dusting

METHOD

MILK MOCHI FILLING Mix all the ingredients except the butter and strain into a heatproof bowl. Steam for 23 – 25 minutes until set.

Transfer to a stand mixer and mix on high speed for 2 minutes using the paddle attachment, then medium speed for 7 – 8 minutes. Add the butter and continue mixing until smooth.

Transfer to a piping bag and chill.

RED BEAN PASTE Place the red beans in a pan and cover with just enough water. Boil for 10 minutes, then drain. Add 500g water to the beans, return to the pot, and boil for another 10 minutes.

Add the light soft brown sugar and cook for 5 minutes, stirring well. Stir in the glucose syrup and salt, then simmer for another 5 minutes, stirring frequently to prevent burning.

Check the consistency – the beans should be very soft and easy to mash. Once cooked, transfer the mixture onto a tray and cover with cling film, pressing it directly onto the surface. Allow to cool, then mash and transfer to a piping bag and store in the fridge.

MATCHA MADELEINE Preheat the oven to 210°C fan (450°F/gas 9) and prepare your mould (page 29).

Melt the butter and milk together in a heatproof bowl over a pan of simmering water, keeping the temperature at 40°C (104°F).

Warm the eggs, sugar and honey to 30°C (86°F).

Mix the dry ingredients gently into the egg mixture, then mix in the butter one-third at a time.

Pipe into the moulds, reduce the oven temperature to 180°C (350°F/gas 4) and bake for 10 – 13 minutes until risen and set.

Remove from the oven, unmould and leave to cool.

MATCHA GLAZE Mix the icing sugar, matcha powder and water until smooth. Use immediately.

TO FINISH Cool completely, then dig out the core using an apple corer and widen slightly with a chopstick. Pipe in the red bean paste (30%) followed by the milk mochi (70%). Replace the core (page 38).

Brush with matcha glaze and let air-dry. Dust the front with the matcha powder just before serving.

MAKES

12

MOULD

Woojung / Chiyoda Madeleine
22mm (5⁄8in) deep

MUGWORT MADELEINES

Mugwort always reminds me of my grandmother making ssuk tteok (mugwort rice cake) for holidays. It's one of our most asked-about flavours, and people often wonder what mugwort is – it's a herbal plant. The flavour is earthy and herbal, almost like a gentler, more fragrant matcha. Many guests are curious at first, but nearly everyone ends up loving it.

INGREDIENTS

MUGWORT BUTTERCREAM

200g (7oz) Swiss buttercream (page 46)
5g (1 tsp) mugwort powder

MUGWORT GLAZE

65g (2¼oz) icing (confectioners') sugar
15g (½oz) water
2.5g (½ tsp) mugwort powder

MUGWORT MADELEINE BATTER

120g cake flour
8g mugwort powder
5g (1 tsp) baking powder
pinch of sea salt
108g unsalted butter
7g (¼oz) milk
85g (3oz) whole eggs, strained (page 31)
80g (2¾oz) caster (superfine) sugar
10g (⅓oz) honey

FOR DECORATION

roasted soybean powder
dates (pitted, rolled and sliced)
toasted pine nuts
pumpkin seeds
glucose syrup

METHOD

MUGWORT BUTTERCREAM Whip the Swiss buttercream with the mugwort powder until fully combined. Set aside.

MUGWORT GLAZE Mix the icing sugar, water and mugwort powder until smooth. Prepare just before use to avoid oxidation. Set aside.

TO BAKE THE MUGWORT MADELEINES Preheat the oven to 210°C fan (230°C/450°F/gas 9) and prepare your mould (page 29).

Sift the flour, baking powder, mugwort powder and salt into a heatproof bowl, then set aside.

Melt the butter and milk together in a heatproof bowl over a pan of simmering water, keeping the temperature at 40°C (104°F).

Warm the eggs, sugar and honey to 30°C (86°F).

Mix the dry ingredients gently into the egg mixture, then mix in the butter one-third at a time.

Pipe into the moulds, reduce the oven temperature to 180°C (350°F/gas 4) and bake for 10 – 13 minutes until risen and set.

Remove from the oven, unmould and leave to cool.

AT THIS POINT, YOU CAN FINISH YOUR MADELEINES IN TWO WAYS:

KEEP IT SIMPLE

Once the madeleines are completely cooled, brush a thin layer of mugwort glaze over the surface and let air-dry.

Dig out the core from the hump side. Fill with mugwort buttercream and cover the hole. Coat the entire surface in roasted soybean powder.

FEELING CONFIDENT? TRY THIS:

Pit, roll and thinly slice the dates. Set aside. Toast the pine nuts in a dry frying pan (skillet), shaking the pan for 2 – 3 minutes until fragrant and lightly golden. Prepare the pumpkin seeds raw or lightly toasted, as preferred.

Once the madeleines are completely cooled, brush a thin layer of mugwort glaze over the surface and let air-dry.

Dig out the core from the front (shell side). Fill with mugwort buttercream and cover the hole with the sliced dates. Decorate with pine nuts and pumpkin seeds using glucose syrup as adhesive.

MAKES

12

MOULD

Woojung / Chiyoda Madeleine 22mm (5/8in) deep

PANDAN & COCONUT MADELEINES

One of our signature flavours, inspired by onde-onde, a beloved Malaysian delicacy. The challenge was making a kaya jam that's soft and rich for the perfect taste, but firm enough to hold inside the sponge. We use Hainanese-style kaya for its deep, caramelized flavour, pairing it with fragrant pandan and toasted coconut for a tropical, comforting bite.

INGREDIENTS

HAINANESE KAYA JAM

95g (3¼oz) palm sugar
300g (10½oz) coconut cream (we use Kara)
115g (4oz) whole eggs, strained (page 31)
20g (⅔oz) caster (superfine) sugar

PANDAN GLAZE

81g (2⅔oz) icing (confectioners') sugar
19g (¾oz) water
1g (pinch) pandan extract

PANDAN MADELEINE BATTER

125g (4½oz) cake flour
5g (1 tsp) baking powder
2g (½ tsp) milk powder
105g (3½oz) unsalted butter
7g (¼oz) milk
85g (3oz) whole eggs, strained (page 31)
80g (2¾oz) caster (superfine) sugar
10g (⅓oz) honey
3g pandan extract
pinch of sea salt

FOR DECORATION

300g (10½oz) desiccated (dried shredded) coconut

METHOD

HAINANESE KAYA JAM In a pan, caramelize the palm sugar to 170°C (340°F). Deglaze by gradually stirring in the coconut cream in three stages and cook until the sugar crystals are fully dissolved, stirring to ensure the mix is even.

Slowly pour into the sieved eggs, stirring constantly. Cook over low heat until it reaches 80°C (175°F), then blend until silky smooth.

Sieve into a container and cover with clingfilm (plastic wrap) touching the surface. Refrigerate until needed.

PANDAN GLAZE Whisk the icing sugar, water and pandan extract until smooth. Set aside.

TO PREP THE DECORATION Toast the desiccated coconut in a dry pan until lightly golden, shaking the pan so it colours evenly. Leave to cool.

PANDAN MADELEINES Preheat the oven to 210°C fan (450°F/gas 9) and prepare your mould (page 29).

Sift the flour, baking powder, milk powder and salt, then set aside.

Melt the butter and milk together in a heatproof bowl over a pan of simmering water, keeping the temperature at 40°C (104°F).

Warm the eggs, caster sugar, honey and pandan extract to 30°C (86°F).

Mix the dry ingredients gently into the egg mixture, then mix in the butter one-third at a time.

Pipe into the moulds, reduce the oven temperature to 180°C (350°F/gas 4) and bake for 10 – 13 minutes until risen and set.

Remove from the oven, unmould and leave to cool.

TO FINISH Once the madeleines are cooled, dig out the core from the hump side. Fill with the kaya jam and replace the core (page 38).

Brush with pandan glaze and roll in toasted coconut to finish.

No one should have to skip dessert. These madeleines are crafted for all – soft, fragrant, and just as satisfying as any classic batch. Sometimes, the best surprises come from trying something a bit different.

DIETARY FRIENDLY

MAKES

12

MOULD

Chiyoda banana

GF CHOCOLATE BANANA MADELEINE

Choco banana is a classic in Japan, loved for its nostalgic mix of rich chocolate and sweet, ripe banana. This madeleine is gluten-free, with a deep cocoa flavour and fresh banana woven into every bite. Soft, moist, and full of comfort, it is proof that gluten-free can still taste like a treat.

INGREDIENTS

BANANA GANACHE

120g (4oz) banana purée
20g (⅔oz) passionfruit purée (optional, can be swapped for same amount of banana purée)
30g (1oz) double (heavy) cream
6g (1½ tsp) milk powder
140g (5oz) white chocolate
20g (⅔oz) cocoa butter
30g (1oz) unsalted butter
1 tsp vanilla paste

GF CHOCOLATE MADELEINE BATTER (12G PER BANANA MOULD / 30 SERVES)

60g (2oz) gluten-free plain (all-purpose) flour
10g (⅓oz) ground almonds
15g (½oz) cocoa (unsweetened chocolate) powder (Dutch-processed), plus extra for dusting
7g (1½ tsp) cornflour (cornstarch)
3g (¾oz) baking powder
pinch of sea salt
100g (3½oz) whole eggs, strained (page 31)
80g (2¾oz) caster (superfine) sugar
15g (½oz) honey
65g (2¼oz) dairy-free butter, plus extra for greasing
20g coconut oil
10g vegetable oil
30g dark chocolate

METHOD

BANANA GANACHE Warm the banana purée, passion fruit purée, cream and vanilla paste in a saucepan.

Melt the chocolate and cocoa butter over a pan of simmering water.

Pour the hot banana mixture over the melted white chocolate and cocoa butter. Stir gently with a spatula to emulsify.

When the ganache cools to 30°C (86°F), add the room-temperature butter and emulsify with a hand blender.

Transfer to a container, cover with clingfilm (plastic wrap) touching the surface, and refrigerate for at least 4 hours to crystallize.

GF CHOCOLATE MADELEINES Preheat the oven to 210°C fan (450°F/gas 9) and prepare your mould.

Sift together the flour, almonds, cocoa powder, cornflour, baking powder and salt. Set aside.

In a bowl, warm the eggs, sugar, and honey to 30°C (86°F). Whisk until combined.

Add the dry ingredients and mix gently for 30 seconds.

In a separate bowl, melt the dairy-free butter, coconut oil, vegetable oil and dark chocolate to 40°C (104°F). Add the warm fat mixture into the batter and whisk for 15 seconds until smooth.

Rest the batter for 30 minutes, or until cooled to 22°C (72°F).

Brush the moulds with melted dairy-free butter and dust lightly with cocoa powder.

Pipe into the moulds, reduce the oven temperature to 180°C fan (400°F/gas 6) for 10 – 12 minutes until risen and set. Let cool completely.

TO FINISH Once cooled, using a piping tip, poke the back of the madeleine three times equally, then pipe in the banana ganache.

Or, simply dip the madeleines into the ganache.

MAKES

30

MOULD

Silicone Small Madeleine
(7cm (l) × 1.7cm (h) × 4.5cm (w),
15g each

VEGAN COCONUT CARAMEL MADELEINE

This madeleine was first created for Market Lane Coffee. It is fully dairy-free but bursting with flavour, with toasted coconut, soft vegan caramel, and a hint of sea salt. You would never guess it was vegan if we didn't tell you. This madeleine is especially meaningful to us, as it became the link between us and our dear friend, and also our photographer, Michael, who captured the spirit of this book so beautifully.

INGREDIENTS

VEGAN COCONUT MADELEINE BATTER

140g (5oz) cake flour
5g (1 tsp) baking powder
pinch of fine salt
½ tsp vanilla paste
15g (½oz) desiccated (dried shredded) coconut, toasted
25g (¾oz) dairy-free butter
25g (¾oz) coconut oil
65g (2¼oz) coconut cream (we use Kara)
80g (2¾oz) aquafaba (chickpea water)
120g (4¼oz) caster (superfine) sugar

DAIRY-FREE MAPLE CARAMEL

75g (2½oz) caster (superfine) sugar
40g (1½oz) coconut cream (we use Kara)
15g (½oz) maple syrup
75g (2½oz) dairy-free butter
pinch of sea salt

CINNAMON GLAZE

130g (4¼oz) icing (confectioners') sugar
1g (pinch) ground cinnamon
30g (1oz) water

FOR DECORATION

desiccated (dried shredded) coconut, for coating

MOULD PREP

neutral oil
semolina powder, for dusting

METHOD

DAIRY-FREE MAPLE CARAMEL Make a dry caramel by gradually melting the caster sugar in a saucepan over low heat until deep amber in colour (170°C/340°F).

Carefully pour in the coconut cream and maple syrup, and stir together to deglaze the pan. Let the mixture come to the boil, then cool to 30°C (86°F).

Add the dairy-free butter and sea salt, then emulsify with a hand blender until smooth and glossy. Set aside.

TO PREPARE THE MOULDS Spray the moulds with neutral oil and dust with semolina powder.

VEGAN COCONUT MADELEINE BATTER Preheat the oven to 210°C fan (450°F/gas 9).

Sift the flour, baking powder and salt. Set aside.

Warm the dairy-free butter, coconut oil and coconut cream together in a heatproof bowl over a pan of simmering water, keeping the temperature at 40°C (104°F).

In a stand mixer, whip the aquafaba until foamy, then add the caster sugar one-third at a time. Continue whipping until the mixture trails off the whisk in ribbons.

Reserve half of the whipped aquafaba and mix the remainder with the warm coconut mixture. Gently fold in the dry ingredients and mix for 30 seconds. Fold in the reserved whipped aquafaba and mix for another 15 seconds until smooth.

Pipe into the prepared moulds, cover the top with another oil-sprayed silicon mould.

Reduce the oven temperature to 180°C (350°F/gas 4) and bake for 12 – 14 minutes until golden and set. Cool completely.

TO FILL THE MADELEINES Once cooled, pipe in the dairy-free maple caramel.

CINNAMON GLAZE & DECORATION Mix the icing sugar, ground cinnamon and water until smooth. Brush both front and back of each madeleine with the glaze.

While the glaze is still tacky, roll each madeleine in desiccated coconut to coat.

I think everyone has that memory of taking a bite of something tangy – your face scrunches up, maybe you laugh, maybe you protest. When I was young, I hated that puckery feeling, but now I love how a bit of sourness can wake up your taste buds. These fruity, vibrant flavours are like little bursts of sunshine: zingy, bright, and just sweet enough to make you smile. They keep desserts feeling light and lively, and somehow, they always bring a bit of fun to the table.

FRUITY & VIBRANT

MAKES

8

MOULD

Woojung / Chiyoda Lemon Shape Mould

LEMON MERINGUE MADELEINES

Our lemon meringue madeleine skips the tart shell and channels a Twinkie vibe instead. Each bite is soft and lemony, with a creamy centre and a swirl of toasted meringue on top. It's light, tangy and full of comfort, reimagining a classic tart as a fun little cake. You will need to start the night before!

INGREDIENTS

LEMON GANACHE

60g (2oz) double (heavy) cream
20g (¾oz) glucose syrup
75g (2½oz) white chocolate
20g (¾oz) unsalted butter
15g (½oz) lemon juice
1.8g (½ tsp) citric acid

LEMON MADELEINE BATTER

125g (4½oz) cake flour
5g (1 tsp) baking powder
pinch of sea salt
105g (3½oz) unsalted butter
7g (¼oz) milk
85g (3oz) whole eggs, strained (page 31)
80g (2¾oz) caster (superfine) sugar
10g (⅓oz) honey
4g grated lemon zest

LEMON GLAZE

65g (2¼oz) icing (confectioners') sugar
7g (¼oz) lemon juice
7g (¼oz) lime juice
lemon or lime zest

FRENCH MERINGUE

65g (2¼oz) egg white
130g (4¼oz) caster sugar
5g (1 tsp) lemon juice

METHOD

LEMON GANACHE Heat the cream and glucose syrup in a pan to 80°C (175°F).

Melt the white chocolate in a plastic bowl in the microwave. Gradually add the hot cream to the chocolate, stirring to emulsify. (Use a hand blender for larger batches.) Cool to 30°C (86°F), then add the butter, lemon juice and citric acid. Mix until smooth and fully combined.

Let crystallize in the fridge overnight.

LEMON MADELEINES Preheat the oven to 210°C fan (450°F/gas 9) and prepare your mould (page 29).

Sift together the flour, baking powder and salt. Set aside.

In a heatproof bowl, melt the butter and milk over a pan of simmering water, keeping the temperature at 40°C (104°F).

Warm the eggs, sugar and honey to 30°C (86°F), then add the grated lemon zest.

Mix the dry ingredients gently into the egg mixture, then mix in the butter one-third at a time.

Pipe into the moulds, reduce the oven temperature to 180°C (350°F/gas 4) and bake for 10 – 13 minutes until risen and set.

Remove from the oven, unmould and leave to cool.

LEMON GLAZE Sift the icing sugar and whisk together with the lemon juice and lime juice until smooth.

TO FILL Once the madeleines are completely cooled, dig out the core from the hump side and fill with lemon ganache. Replace the removed core (page 38).

AT THIS POINT, YOU CAN FINISH YOUR MADELEINES IN TWO WAYS:

KEEP IT SIMPLE

Brush the front with lemon glaze and dry in the oven at 130°C fan (320°F/gas 2) for 1 minute, then let air-dry at room temperature. Finish with grated lemon or lime zest.

FEELING CONFIDENT? TRY THIS:

FRENCH MERINGUE Whip the egg whites in a stand mixer on medium speed until foamy. Gradually add the caster sugar in three additions, whipping well after each. Increase to high speed and continue whipping until stiff peaks form and the meringue is glossy. Use immediately.

TO FINISH Dip the hump of the madeleine into the French meringue. Torch lightly with a blow torch and finish with grated lemon or lime zest.

TIP Any leftover meringue can be spread on a tray with baking or parchment paper, and dehydrated to make a meringue shard.

MAKES

12

MOULD

Woojung / Chiyoda Madeleine 22mm (5⁄8in) deep

MOJITO MADELEINES

Inspired by one of my favourite cocktails, these madeleines bring together lime, mint and just a touch of rum. They're bright, cool and a little bit boozy – perfect for summer parties or anytime you want a taste of sunshine. They turn any ordinary day into a mini summer holiday. Start night before.

INGREDIENTS

MOJITO GANACHE

40g (1½oz) double (heavy) cream
20g (¾oz) glucose syrup
80g (2¾oz) white chocolate
15g (½oz) unsalted butter
5g (1 tsp) lemon juice
5g (1 tsp) lime juice
20g (¾oz) white rum
pinch of citric acid
a few drops of mint extract

LIME MADELEINE BATTER

125g (4½oz) cake flour
5g (1 tsp) baking powder
pinch of sea salt
105g (3½oz) unsalted butter
7g (¼oz) milk
85g (3oz) whole eggs, strained (page 31)
80g (2¾oz) caster (superfine) sugar
10g (⅓oz) honey
3g (¾ tsp) lime zest

MOJITO GLAZE (100G)

83g (3oz) icing (confectioners') sugar
9g (⅜oz) lemon juice
9g (⅜oz) lime zest

GREEN LIME CHOCOLATE

200g (7oz) white chocolate
a few drops of fat-soluble yellow food colouring
a few drops of fat-soluble green food colouring

METHOD

MOJITO GANACHE Warm the cream and glucose syrup in a pan to 80°C (175°F). Pour over the white chocolate and emulsify with a hand blender. Cool down to 30°C (86°F), then add the butter, lemon juice, lime juice, white rum, citric acid and mint extract. Blend again until fully smooth.

Transfer to a container and let crystallize in the fridge overnight.

LIME MADELEINES Preheat the oven to 210°C fan (450°F/gas 9) and prepare your mould (page 29).

Sift together the flour, baking powder and salt. Set aside.

Melt the butter and milk together in a heatproof bowl over a pan of simmering water, keeping the temperature at 40°C (104°F).

Warm the eggs, sugar, honey and lime zest to 30°C (86°F).

Mix the dry ingredients gently into the egg mixture, then mix in the butter one-third at a time.

Pipe into the moulds, reduce the oven temperature to 180°C (350°F/gas 4) and bake for 10 – 13 minutes until risen and set.

Remove from the oven, unmould and leave to cool.

MOJITO GLAZE Sift the icing sugar, then add the lemon and lime juices and whisk until smooth.

TO FILL Once cooled, dig out the core from the hump side of each madeleine and fill with mojito ganache. Brush the front with mojito glaze and let air-dry at room temperature.

AT THIS POINT, YOU CAN FINISH YOUR MADELEINES IN TWO WAYS:

KEEP IT SIMPLE

Garnish with lime zest.

FEELING CONFIDENT? TRY THIS:

TO FINISH WITH GREEN LIME CHOCOLATE Use tempered green-coloured white chocolate to stencil lime shapes and apply as a garnish.

MAKES

12

MOULD

Woojung / Chiyoda Madeleine 22mm (5⁄8in) deep

PASSIONFRUIT PAVLOVA MADELEINES

For me, this madeleine captures that first bite of pavlova on a warm summer day. The shell shatters with a crunch, giving way to silky passionfruit curd and a light, buttery sponge. The passionfruit lifts everything – sweet, fragrant, and tart at once. It's still a little strange to have Christmas in the heat after growing up with winter holidays, but pavlova has become one of my favourite Aussie traditions. Each bite is pure sunshine, all wrapped up in a soft cake.

INGREDIENTS

PASSIONFRUIT CURD

1g (¼ tsp) gelatine leaf
70g (2½oz) caster (superfine) sugar
130g (4½oz) whole eggs, strained (page 31)
80g (2¾oz) passionfruit purée
20g (⅔oz) orange juice
50g (1¾oz) unsalted butter

PASSIONFRUIT GLAZE

65g (2¼oz) icing (confectioners') sugar
15g (½oz) passionfruit juice

LEMON MADELEINE BATTER

125g (4½oz) cake flour
5g (1 tsp) baking powder
pinch of sea salt
105g (3½oz) unsalted butter
7g (¼oz) milk
85g (3oz) whole eggs, strained (page 31)
80g (2¾oz) caster (superfine) sugar
10g (⅓oz) honey
3g (¾ tsp) grated lemon zest

MERINGUE SHARD

125g (4½oz) caster (superfine) sugar
65g (2¼oz) egg whites
10g (⅓oz) passionfruit juice

METHOD

PASSIONFRUIT CURD Soften the gelatine leaf in iced water.

In a saucepan, whisk together the sugar, eggs, passionfruit purée and orange juice. Cook over low heat, stirring constantly, to 82°C (180°F) until thickened. Remove from heat and whisk in the softened gelatine.

Cool slightly, then mix in the butter until smooth. Strain, transfer to a container and chill until set.

PASSIONFRUIT GLAZE Sift the icing sugar, then mix with the passionfruit juice until smooth. Use immediately or cover the surface with clingfilm (plastic wrap) to prevent crystallisation.

LEMON MADELEINES Preheat the oven to 210°C fan (450°F/gas 9) and prepare your mould (page 29).

Sift the flour, baking powder and salt, then set aside.

Melt the butter and milk together in a heatproof bowl over a pan of simmering water, keeping the temperature at 40°C (104°F).

Warm the eggs, sugar and honey to 30°C (86°F).

Mix the dry ingredients gently into the egg mixture, then mix in the butter one-third at a time.

Pipe into the moulds, reduce the oven temperature to 180°C (350°F/gas 4) and bake for 10 – 13 minutes until risen and set.

Remove from the oven, unmould and leave to cool.

TO FILL AND GLAZE Once fully cooled, dig out the core from the belly side of each madeleine. Fill with the passionfruit curd and replace the trimmed core (page 38).

Brush the top with passionfruit glaze and let air-dry.

AT THIS POINT, YOU CAN FINISH YOUR MADELEINES IN TWO WAYS:

KEEP IT SIMPLE

Garnish with pieces of store-bought pavlova or skip the meringue shard entirely. Drizzle fresh passionfruit pulp over just before serving.

FEELING CONFIDENT? TRY THIS:

MERINGUE SHARD Preheat the oven to 85°C fan (220°F/gas ¼) and line a baking sheet with baking parchment, and spray some oil lightly to prevent sticking.

Using a stand mixer, whip the egg whites until frothy. Gradually add sugar one-third at a time, whipping until stiff glossy peaks form.

Add the passionfruit juice and mix briefly to combine. Spread onto the prepared tray and bake for 2 hours until completely dry and crisp. Let cool, then break into shards. Store in an airtight container.

TO FINISH Garnish each madeleine with a meringue shard by sticking with passionfruit curd just before serving. Drizzle fresh passionfruit pulp over.

MAKES

12

MOULD

Woojung / Chiyoda Madeleine 22mm (⅝in) deep

PEACH MELBA MADELEINES

This madeleine was created for our Piper-Heidsieck collaboration during the Australian Open. Inside the citrus base is a mix of white peach and raspberry jam blended with Champagne jelly. Covered in chocolate enrobage, it brings together the flavours of summer, ripe fruit and celebration, all at once.

INGREDIENTS

CHAMPAGNE JELLY

7g (¼oz) gelatine leaf
150g (5¼oz) Champagne
15g (½oz) caster (superfine) sugar
5g (1 tsp) lemon juice

RASPBERRY JAM

100g (3 ¼oz) raspberry purée
50g (1¾oz) caster (superfine) sugar
50g (1¾oz) glucose syrup
5g (1 tsp) lemon juice

WHITE PEACH COMPOTE

150g (5¼oz) white peach purée
75g (2⅝oz) glucose syrup
75g (2⅝oz) caster (superfine) sugar
5g (⅛oz) lemon juice

VANILLA MADELEINE BATTER

125g (4½oz) cake flour
5g (1 tsp) baking powder
pinch of sea salt
105g (3½oz) unsalted butter
7g (¼oz) milk
85g (3oz) whole eggs, strained (page 31)
80g (2¾oz) caster (superfine) sugar
10g (⅓oz) honey
½ tsp vanilla paste
3g (¾ tsp) grated lemon zest

CHAMPAGNE PEACH MELBA FILLING RATIO

white peach compote 70%
raspberry jam 20%
Champagne jelly 10%

RED ENROBAGE

250g (9oz) white chocolate
60g (2oz) cocoa butter
10g (⅓oz) grapeseed oil
10g (⅓oz) 56% dark chocolate
5g (1 tsp) red fat-soluble food colouring

FOR DECORATION

white chocolate (for tennis ball lines)
gold leaf (optional)

METHOD

CHAMPAGNE JELLY Soften the gelatine leaf in iced water.

Warm one-third of the Champagne with the sugar in a small pan. Add the softened gelatine and stir to dissolve. Add the remaining Champagne and the lemon juice and mix well. Strain and refrigerate until set.

RASPBERRY JAM Combine the raspberry purée, sugar and glucose syrup in a pan. Boil over medium-high heat for 15 minutes, skimming off any foam that rises to the surface. Check consistency by dropping a small spoonful into cold water – if it holds its shape and doesn't spread, it's ready. Add lemon juice. Let cool completely.

WHITE PEACH COMPOTE Combine the peach purée, glucose syrup and sugar in a pan. Boil over medium-high heat, stirring constantly, until reduced by half. Test the consistency by dropping into cold water – it should hold its shape. Stir in the lemon juice. Let cool.

VANILLA MADELEINE Preheat the oven to 210°C fan (450°F/gas 9) and prepare your mould (page 29).

Sift the flour, baking powder and salt, then set aside.

Melt the butter and milk together in a heatproof bowl over a pan of simmering water, keeping the temperature at 40°C (104°F).

Warm the eggs, sugar, honey, vanilla paste and lemon zest to 30°C (86°F).

Mix the dry ingredients gently into the egg mixture, then mix in the butter one-third at a time.

Pipe into the moulds, reduce the oven temperature to 180°C (350°F/gas 4) and bake for 10 – 13 minutes until risen and set.

Remove from the oven, unmould and leave to cool.

Prepare the filling by combining 70% peach compote, 20% raspberry jam and 10% Champagne jelly. Blend until smooth. Dig out the core from the belly side of each cooled madeleine. Fill with the blended fruit filling and replace the removed lid (page 38).

AT THIS POINT, YOU CAN FINISH YOUR MADELEINES IN TWO WAYS:

KEEP IT SIMPLE

Serve as is, or garnish with a dusting of icing sugar or gold leaf, if desired.

FEELING CONFIDENT? TRY THIS:

BEFORE YOU BEGIN:

Insert a skewer into the base of each filled madeleine and freeze for at least 4 hours until fully frozen.

RED ENROBAGE When the madeleines are frozen, melt the white chocolate, cocoa butter, grapeseed oil and dark chocolate together. Add the red colouring and emulsify with a hand blender. Maintain at 32°C (90°F) for dipping.

TO FINISH Dip each frozen madeleine into the red enrobage and leave to set in the freezer.

Pipe tennis ball lines using tempered white chocolate (page 42).

STRAWBERRY MADELEINES

MAKES

12

MOULD

Woojung / Chiyoda Madeleine 22mm (⅝in) deep

Who doesn't love strawberry? These madeleines are all about letting the fruit do the talking: strawberry jam and a glaze made from puréed berries. Every bite is soft, delicate, and alive with that fresh-picked taste.

INGREDIENTS

STRAWBERRY JAM

150g (5¼oz) strawberries, diced and mashed
150g (5¼oz) caster (superfine) sugar
10g (⅓oz) lemon juice

STRAWBERRY GLAZE

25g (¾oz) strawberry purée
60g (2oz) icing (confectioners') sugar
7g (¼oz) olive oil
3g (¾ tsp) lemon juice

LEMON MADELEINE BATTER

125g (4½oz) cake flour
5g (1 tsp) baking powder
pinch of sea salt
105g (3½oz) unsalted butter
7g (¼oz) milk
85g (3oz) whole eggs, strained (page 31)
80g (2¾oz) caster (superfine) sugar
10g (⅓oz) honey
3g (¾ tsp) grated lemon zest

FOR DECORATION

Sosa yogurt crisps or chopped white chocolate

METHOD

STRAWBERRY JAM Wash ripe strawberries, remove the tops, and dice them.

Mix the strawberries with the sugar and place in a pan.

Cook over medium heat for 10 – 15 minutes, stirring occasionally.

Skim off any foam that rises to the top to ensure a clear jam. Check consistency by dropping a small spoonful into cold water – if it holds its shape and doesn't spread, it's ready.

Add lemon juice and stir through. Let cool fully.

STRAWBERRY GLAZE Mix the strawberry purée, icing sugar, olive oil and lemon juice together until smooth. Set aside.

LEMON MADELEINES Preheat the oven to 210°C fan (410°F/gas 7) and prepare your mould (page 29).

Sift the flour, baking powder and salt, then set aside.

Melt the butter and milk together in a heatproof bowl over a pan of simmering water, keeping the temperature at 40°C (104°F).

Warm the eggs, sugar, honey and lemon zest to 30°C (86°F).

Mix the dry ingredients gently into the egg mixture, then mix in the butter one-third at a time.

Pipe into the moulds, reduce the oven temperature to 180°C (350°F/gas 4) and bake for 10 – 13 minutes until risen and set.

TO FINISH Once the madeleines are completely cooled, pipe the strawberry jam into the belly side using a jam nozzle. Brush or spoon the strawberry glaze over the surface of the madeleine. Place in the oven at 130°C fan (300°F/gas 2) for 1 minute to partially set the glaze. Flip and dry the other side and repeat for 1 min.

Finish with Sosa yogurt crisps and/or chopped white chocolate pressed gently onto the glaze before it sets.

I have a soft spot for anything rich and chocolatey. Give me chocolate, roasted nuts, something rich and creamy or a little crunch, and I'm happy. These are the kinds of madeleines that remind me of my childhood – when my dad, after a night out, would come home with a bag full of snacks he knew we loved (like chocolate pies, cookies, or a Ghana chocolate bar). I never really had the habit of eating late at night, so I'd squirrel them away in my drawer – the one with a lock my dad made just for me (because, as you know if you have siblings...) – and save them for later. Just knowing they were there made me happy, and when I finally opened the drawer, it felt like my own tiny celebration.

INDULGENT

BLACK FOREST MADELEINES

MAKES

12

MOULD

Woojung / Chiyoda Madeleine
22mm (⅝in) deep

Black Forest gateaux has always felt like the ultimate treat for me. Rich chocolate, sweet-tart cherry, and a creamy finish come together here in a madeleine: soft chocolate sponge, tangy cherry jam, and a smooth vanilla ganache at the centre. Every bite is lush and nostalgic. Start night before.

INGREDIENTS

CHERRY SYRUP
25g (¾oz) caster (superfine) sugar
10g (⅓oz) water
15g (½oz) cherry purée

VANILLA GANACHE
120g double (heavy) UHT cream
½ tsp vanilla paste
30g glucose syrup
166g white chocolate
18g unsalted butter

CHERRY JAM
150g (5¼oz) cherry purée
150g (5¼oz) caster (superfine) sugar
10g (⅓oz) lemon juice

CHOCOLATE GLAZE
85g (3oz) icing (confectioners') sugar
5g (1 tsp) cocoa (unsweetened chocolate) powder (Dutch-processed)
25g (¾oz) water

CHOCOLATE MADELEINE BATTER
110g (3¾oz) cake flour
15g (1 tsp) cocoa (unsweetened chocolate) powder (Dutch-processed)
5g (1 tsp) baking powder
105g (3½oz) unsalted butter
7g (¼oz) milk
85g (3oz) whole eggs, strained (page 31)
80g (2¾oz) caster (superfine) sugar
10g (⅓oz) honey
pinch of sea salt

RED CHERRY CHOCOLATE
250g (9oz) white chocolate
50g (1¾oz) dark chocolate
5g (1 tsp) red fat-soluble food colouring powder (use with a cherry-shaped stencil)

METHOD

CHERRY SYRUP Combine the sugar, water and cherry purée in a pan. Bring to the boil over medium heat. Remove from heat and set aside to cool.

VANILLA GANACHE Warm the cream, vanilla paste and glucose syrup in a pan to 80°C (175°F). Pour over the white chocolate and emulsify with a hand blender. Cool down to 30°C (86°F), then add room temperature butter in small pieces. Hand blend again until fully smooth.

Transfer to a container and let crystallize in the fridge overnight.

CHERRY JAM Combine the cherry purée and sugar in a pan and bring to a boil. Cook over medium heat for 10 – 15 minutes, stirring occasionally.

Skim off any foam that rises to the top to ensure a clear jam.

Check consistency by dropping a small spoonful into cold water – if it holds its shape and doesn't spread, it's ready.

Add lemon juice and stir through. Let cool fully.

CHOCOLATE GLAZE Sift the icing sugar and cocoa powder into a bowl. Add the water and whisk until smooth. Use immediately or cover with clingfilm (plastic wrap) touching the surface.

CHOCOLATE MADELEINES Preheat the oven to 210°C fan (450°F/gas 9) and prepare your mould (page 29).

Sift the flour, cocoa powder, baking powder and salt into a heatproof bowl, then set aside.

Melt the butter and milk together in a heatproof bowl over a pan of simmering water, keeping the temperature at 40°C (104°F).

Warm the eggs, sugar and honey to 30°C (86°F).

Mix the dry ingredients gently into the egg mixture, then mix in the butter one-third at a time.

Pipe into the moulds, reduce the oven temperature to 180°C (350°F/gas 4) and bake for 10 – 13 minutes until risen and set.

Remove from the oven, unmould and leave to cool.

AT THIS POINT, YOU CAN FINISH YOUR MADELEINES IN TWO WAYS:

KEEP IT SIMPLE

Once cooled, brush the madeleines with cherry syrup.Dig out the core from the belly side and fill with cherry jam, followed by vanilla ganache. Replace the removed core (page 38).

Brush the front with a thin layer of chocolate glaze and let it air-dry.

FEELING CONFIDENT? TRY THIS:

CHERRY CHOCOLATE Melt the white and dark chocolate together.

Add the red food colouring and mix until evenly coloured and temper (page 42). Spread over a cherry-shaped stencil and let crystallize at room temperature.

TO FINISH Melt some of the red cherry chocolate and use it to stick the cherry chocolate on. Let it set at room temperature for a couple of minutes. Decorate each madeleine with a red cherry chocolate to finish.

MAKES

12

MOULD

Chiyoda Scallop Shell

EVOO CHOCOLATE MADELEINES

Dark chocolate and extra virgin olive oil are a perfect match you might not expect. The floral and fruity notes of the oil bring out a new depth in the chocolate. The sponge is moist and light, with a silky olive oil ganache at the centre. Each bite has a gentle richness, a bright aroma, and a lingering finish that is both comforting and surprising.

INGREDIENTS

OLIVE CHOCOLATE GLAZE

85g (3oz) icing (confectioners') sugar
15g (½oz) water
10g (⅓oz) extra virgin olive oil
5g (1 tsp) cocoa (unsweetened chocolate) powder (Dutch-processed)

CHOCOLATE MADELEINE BATTER

110g (3¾oz) cake flour
15g (½oz) cocoa (unsweetened chocolate) powder (Dutch-processed)
5g (1 tsp) baking powder
pinch of sea salt
105g (3½oz) unsalted butter
7g (¼oz) milk
85g (3oz) whole eggs, strained (page 31)
80g (2¾oz) caster (superfine) sugar
10g (⅓oz) honey

DARK CHOCOLATE OLIVE OIL GANACHE

65g (2½oz) double (heavy) cream
20g (⅔oz) glucose syrup
65g (2¼oz) 53% dark chocolate (we use Sakanti Bali from Valrhona)
½ tsp ascorbic acid (optional)
50g (1¾oz) good-quality extra virgin olive oil
pinch of sea salt

FOR DECORATION

gold leaf
cocoa powder, optional

METHOD

DARK CHOCOLATE OLIVE OIL GANACHE Warm the cream and glucose syrup together until just simmering. Pour over the chopped dark chocolate and blend with a hand blender until emulsified. Add salt and ascorbic acid and mix well.

Once the ganache temperature drops to 35 – 40°C (95 – 104°F), slowly stream in the olive oil while hand-mixing to create a smooth, shiny emulsion. Transfer to a piping bag and let crystallize in the fridge until ready to use.

OLIVE CHOCOLATE GLAZE Sift the icing sugar and cocoa powder together. Add the water and olive oil, then whisk until smooth and glossy. Keep aside with cling film over to prevent crystallisation.

CHOCOLATE MADELEINES Preheat the oven to 210°C fan (450°F/gas 9) and prepare your mould (page 29).

Sift the flour, baking powder, cocoa powder and salt, then set aside.

Melt the butter and milk together in a heatproof bowl over a pan of simmering water, keeping the temperature at 40°C (104°F).

Warm the eggs, sugar and honey to 30°C (86°F).

Mix the dry ingredients gently into the egg mixture, then mix in the butter one-third at a time.

Pipe into the moulds, reduce the oven temperature to 180°C (350°F/gas 4) and bake for 10 – 13 minutes until risen and set.

Remove from the oven, unmould and leave to cool.

TO FINISH Once the madeleines are baked and cooled, dig out the core from the belly side and fill with dark chocolate olive oil ganache. Replace the removed core to seal (page 38).

Brush the surface of each madeleine with olive chocolate glaze (page 41). Let air-dry at room temperature until the glaze is set.

Gently apply gold leaf as a final decoration. Alternatively, you can cover the whole madeleine with cocoa powder.

MAKES

12

MOULD

Woojung / Chiyoda Madeleine 22mm (⅝in) deep

EARL GREY MADELEINE

I first learned the beauty of tea culture in the UK, where a cup of Earl Grey is often part of the day. It quickly became my favourite, and now it's at the heart of our top-selling madeleine. The citrus notes of Earl Grey pair perfectly with Dulcey chocolate's caramel warmth, making every bite feel like Afternoon Tea in a single mouthful. Start night before.

INGREDIENTS

DULCEY EARL GREY GANACHE

170g (6oz) double (heavy) cream
6g (2 tsp) Earl Grey tea leaves, finely blended
160g (5½oz) caramelized white chocolate (Dulcey from Valrhona)
30g (1oz) glucose syrup
10g (⅓oz) unsalted butter

EARL GREY MADELEINE BATTER

105g (3½oz) unsalted butter
7g (¼oz) milk
85g (3oz) whole eggs, strained (page 31)
80g (2¾oz) caster (superfine) sugar
10g (⅓oz) honey
3g (¾ tsp) lemon zest
125g (4½oz) cake flour
3g (¾ tsp) Earl Grey tea powder, finely blended
5g (1 tsp) baking powder
pinch of sea salt

EARL GREY SYRUP

25g (¾oz) caster (superfine) sugar
10g (⅓oz) water
pinch of Earl Grey tea leaves
15g (½oz) lemon juice

EARL GREY GLAZE

65g (2¼oz) icing (confectioners') sugar
pinch of Earl Grey tea powder
15g (½oz) water

DULCEY CHOCOLATE SHELL

300g (10½oz) caramelized white chocolate (Dulcey from Valrhona)

FOR DECORATION

dried cornflower
glucose syrup (for attaching decoration)

METHOD

DULCEY EARL GREY GANACHE Heat the cream and Earl Grey tea in a pan to 80°C (175°F). Let steep for 5 minutes.

Strain the tea leaves and reheat the infused cream (some fine tea powder may remain). Pour over the Dulcey chocolate and glucose sugar and emulsify gently with a hand blender.

Cool to 30°C (86°F), then add the room temperature butter and blend again. Transfer to a container and press clingfilm (plastic wrap) directly onto the surface. Let crystallize overnight in the fridge.

EARL GREY SYRUP Combine the sugar, water and Earl Grey tea leaves in a pan and bring to the boil. Remove from the heat and let steep for 5 minutes. Strain, then mix in the lemon juice and let cool completely.

EARL GREY MADELEINES Preheat the oven to 210°C fan (450°F/gas 9) and prepare your mould (page 29).

Sift the flour, tea powder, baking powder and salt, then set aside.

Melt the butter and milk together in a heatproof bowl over a pan of simmering water, keeping the temperature at 40°C (104°F).

Warm the eggs, sugar, honey and lemon zest to 30°C (86°F).

Mix the dry ingredients gently into the egg mixture, then mix in the butter one-third at a time.

Pipe into the moulds, reduce the oven temperature to 180°C (350°F/gas 4) and bake for 10 – 13 minutes until risen and set.

Remove from the oven, unmould and leave to cool.

EARL GREY GLAZE Sift the icing sugar and Earl Grey tea powder. Add the water gradually and whisk until smooth.

AT THIS POINT, YOU CAN FINISH YOUR MADELEINES IN TWO WAYS:

KEEP IT SIMPLE

Once the madeleines are completely cooled, glaze the whole madeleine and let dry.

Dig out the core from the hump and fill with Dulcey Earl Grey ganache.

Replace the removed core to seal.

Attach dried cornflower petals with glucose syrup.

FEELING CONFIDENT? TRY THIS:

Glaze thinly the hump side only and dry it.

Dig out the core from the front (shell side) and fill with Dulcey Earl Grey ganache.

Temper the Dulcey chocolate (page 42) and pour 15g (½oz) into each mould cavity.

Gently press the glazed madeleine into the mould and let it set at room temperature for at least 4 hours (or set at room temp for 1 hour and keep in the fridge for 10 mins, and check, as metal mould in the fridge might cool down too fast and chocolate shell might crack). Lightly cover the mould to prevent drying out.

Once fully set, carefully unmould.

Attach dried cornflower petals using glucose syrup.

HAZELNUT ROCHER MADELEINES

MAKES

12

MOULD

Woojung / Chiyoda Madeleine 22mm (⅝in) deep

Inspired by Ferrero Rocher, this madeleine is all about texture and richness. Each one is enrobed in crunchy hazelnut and milk chocolate. Inside, there's a whipped hazelnut ganache and a layer of gooey salted caramel. It's nutty, creamy, and indulgent – like your favourite chocolate, but even more decadent. Start night before.

INGREDIENTS

HAZELNUT WHIPPED GANACHE

160g (5½oz) double (heavy) cream
40g (1½oz) glucose syrup
30g (1oz) milk chocolate, chopped
65g (2¼oz) hazelnut paste
225g (8oz) double (heavy) cream, cold
pinch of sea salt

SALTED CARAMEL

100g (3¼oz) caster (superfine) sugar
50g (1¾oz) double (heavy) cream
60g (2oz) unsalted butter
pinch of sea salt

BROWN BUTTER MADELEINE BATTER

125g (4½oz) cake flour
3g (¾ tsp) caramelized milk powder
5g (1 tsp) baking powder
pinch of sea salt
104g unsalted butter
7g (¼oz) milk
85g (3oz) whole eggs, strained (page 31)
80g (2¾oz) caster (superfine) sugar
10g (⅓oz) Leatherwood honey

FOR BRUSHING

30g (1oz) espresso

ENROBAGE

300g (10½oz) milk chocolate
300g (10½oz) cocoa butter
50g (1¾oz) hazelnuts, roasted and crushed

DECORATION

edible gold powder

METHOD

HAZELNUT WHIPPED GANACHE Heat the cream and glucose syrup until steaming. Pour over the milk chocolate and emulsify with a hand blender. Add the hazelnut paste and salt. Blend again until smooth. Slowly stream in the cold cream and emulsify until glossy.

Cover with clingfilm (plastic wrap) touching the surface and refrigerate overnight. Whip to soft peaks before use.

SALTED CARAMEL In a dry saucepan, caramelize the sugar in stages until amber. Deglaze with the warm cream and stir until smooth. Add the butter and sea salt, then emulsify.

Cool, transfer to a piping bag and refrigerate.

BROWN BUTTER MADELEINES Preheat the oven to 210°C fan (450°F/gas 9) and prepare your mould (page 29).

Sift the flour, baking powder, caramelized milk powder and salt, then set aside.

Melt the butter and milk together in a heatproof bowl over a pan of simmering water, keeping the temperature at 40°C (104°F).

Warm the eggs, sugar and honey to 30°C (86°F).

Mix the dry ingredients gently into the egg mixture, then mix in the butter one-third at a time.

Pipe into the moulds, reduce the oven temperature to 180°C (350°F/gas 4) and bake for 10 – 13 minutes until risen and set.

Remove from the oven, unmould and leave to cool slightly.

AT THIS POINT, YOU CAN FINISH YOUR MADELEINES IN TWO WAYS:

KEEP IT SIMPLE

Once cooled, dig out the core from the belly side of each madeleine. Fill each with salted caramel, then top with hazelnut whipped ganache. Replace the core (page 38).

Chill in the fridge until set.

FEELING CONFIDENT? TRY THIS:

Once cooled, dig out the core from the belly side of each madeleine. Fill each with salted caramel, then top with hazelnut whipped ganache. Replace the core. Lightly brush with espresso, freeze for at least 4 hours.

ROCHER ENROBAGE Melt the milk chocolate and cocoa butter together and bring to 31°C (88°F). Stir in the crushed hazelnuts and keep warm.

FINISHING Skewer the madeleines. Dip the whole madeleine into the rocher enrobage and set upright in a chocolate setting dock (page 41). Chill in the fridge for at least 15 minutes.

Once fully set, remove from skewers and brush the chocolate shell lightly with gold powder to finish.

MAKES

12

MOULD

Woojung / Chiyoda Madeleine 22mm (⅝in) deep

PISTA BLUSH MADELEINES

Pistachio and raspberry are a dream pairing – rich, nutty and just the right amount of tart. We roast and grind our own pistachios into a silky paste for the batter, then balance that creamy depth with a bright raspberry centre. Every bite is soft and luxurious, with a pop of tang that keeps it light.

INGREDIENTS

RASPBERRY JAM

100g (3¼oz) raspberry purée
50g (1¾oz) sugar
50g (1¾oz) glucose syrup
5g (1 tsp) lemon juice

PISTACHIO BUTTERCREAM

50g pistachio paste
100g (3¼oz) Swiss buttercream (page 46)

ORANGE PISTACHIO MADELEINE BATTER

120g (4¼oz) cake flour
5g (1 tsp) baking powder
pinch of sea salt
80g (2¾oz) unsalted butter
30g (1oz) pistachio paste
25g (1oz) grapeseed oil
7g (¼oz) milk
85g (3oz) whole eggs, strained (page 31)
80g (2¾oz) caster (superfine) sugar
10g (⅓oz) honey
3g (¾ tsp) orange zest

PISTACHIO ENROBAGE

150g (5¼oz) white chocolate
35g (1¼oz) cocoa butter
15g (½oz) pistachio paste
15g (½oz) pistachios, crushed
10g (⅓oz) almonds, silvered or crushed
5g (1 tsp) dried rose petals
15g (½oz) grapeseed oil

DECORATION

white chocolate
crushed pistachio

METHOD

RASPBERRY JAM Combine the raspberry purée and sugar in a pan and bring to the boil. Cook over medium heat for 10 – 15 minutes, stirring occasionally.

Skim off any foam that rises to the top to ensure a clear jam.

Check the consistency by dropping a small spoonful into cold water – if it holds its shape and doesn't spread, it's ready.

Add the lemon juice and stir through. Let cool fully.

PISTACHIO BUTTERCREAM Whip the pistachio paste and Swiss buttercream together until smooth. Transfer to a piping bag and set aside.

MADELEINES Preheat the oven to 210°C fan (450°F/gas 9) and prepare your mould (page 29).

Sift the flour, baking powder and salt, then set aside.

Melt the butter, pistachio paste, oil and milk together in a heatproof bowl over a pan of simmering water, keeping the temperature at 40°C (104°F).

Warm the eggs, sugar, honey and orange zest to 30°C (86°F).

Mix the dry ingredients gently into the egg mixture, then mix in the butter one-third at a time.

Pipe into the moulds, reduce the oven temperature to 180°C (350°F/gas 4) and bake for 10 – 13 minutes until risen and set.

Remove from the oven, unmould and leave to cool.

AT THIS POINT, YOU CAN FINISH YOUR MADELEINES IN TWO WAYS:

KEEP IT SIMPLE

Dig out the core from the belly side of each madeleine. Fill with pistachio buttercream and raspberry jam. Replace the core (page 38).

Optional – dip the front (shell side) with melted white chocolate (about 30°C, no tempering needed) and sprinkle with crushed pistachio.

FEELING CONFIDENT? TRY THIS:

Dig out the core from the belly side of each madeleine. Fill with pistachio buttercream and raspberry jam. Replace the core.

Insert a skewer and freeze for at least 4 hours.

PISTACHIO ENROBAGE Melt the white chocolate, cocoa butter and pistachio paste together and emulsify with a hand blender. Stir in the crushed pistachio, almonds, rose petals and grapeseed oil. Maintain at 35°C (95°F) for dipping.

FINISHING Dip the whole madeleine into the pistachio enrobage and set upright in a chocolate setting dock (page 41). Chill in the fridge for at least 15 minutes.

Once fully set, remove from skewers.

I personally think the beauty of being a pastry chef is getting to make someone's moment feel a little more special and memorable. These flavours may only appear once a year, and maybe that's why they feel so precious. They take more time and care, but I love how they still manage to surprise people. Some are playful, some are made with a lot of heart. Each one has its own story. I just hope they stay with people, even after the last bite.

SEASONAL & CELEBRATION

MAKES

12

MOULD

Matsunaga Bear Madeleine

GINGER BEAR MADELEINE

This is our take on the classic gingerbread man – cute, spiced and a little bit playful. Each madeleine is warmly spiced, filled with creamy Speculoos ganache, and coated in silky Dulcey chocolate. As they bake, the kitchen fills with the scent of ginger, cinnamon, and caramel. We even have a customer with diabetes who tells us they can resist most sweets, but always make an exception for our ginger bear. Whether you use a bear mould or not, this recipe bakes up soft, spiced, and impossible to resist. Start night before.

INGREDIENTS

SPECULOOS GANACHE

100g (3¼oz) double (heavy) cream
40g (1½oz) caramelized white chocolate (we use Dulcey from Valrhona)
50g (1¾oz) lotus biscoff
3g (¾ tsp) gingerbread spice
pinch of sea salt

CINNAMON GLAZE

65g (2¼oz) icing (confectioners') sugar
15g (½oz) water
pinch of ground cinnamon

GINGERBREAD MADELEINE BATTER

120g (4¼oz) cake flour
5g (1 tsp) baking powder
5g (1 tsp) gingerbread spice
3g (½ tsp) grated orange zest
pinch of sea salt
100g (3¼oz) unsalted butter
7g (¼oz) milk
80g (2¾oz) whole eggs, strained (page 31)
75g (2½oz) caster (superfine) sugar
10g (⅓oz) honey

FOR DECORATION

25g (¾oz) white chocolate
300g (10½oz) caramelized white chocolate (Dulcey from Valrhona)

METHOD

SPECULOOS GANACHE Warm the cream to 80°C (175°F). Pour over the chocolate and stir until smooth and emulsified.

Add the crushed lotus biscoff, gingerbread spice and sea salt. Blend well. Cover with clingfilm (plastic wrap) touching the surface and refrigerate overnight.

CINNAMON GLAZE Sift the icing sugar into a bowl. Add the water and cinnamon and whisk until smooth. Set aside.

GINGERBREAD MADELEINES Preheat the oven to 210°C fan (450°F/gas 9) and prepare your mould (page 29).

Sift the flour, baking powder, gingerbread spice and salt, then set aside.

Melt the butter and milk together in a heatproof bowl over a pan of simmering water, keeping the temperature at 40°C (104°F).

Warm the eggs, sugar, orange zest and honey to 30°C (86°F).

Mix the dry ingredients gently into the egg mixture, then mix in the butter one-third at a time.

Pipe into the moulds, reduce the oven temperature to 180°C (350°F/gas 4) and bake for 10 – 13 minutes until risen and set.

Remove from the oven, unmould and leave to cool.

AT THIS POINT, YOU CAN FINISH YOUR MADELEINES IN TWO WAYS:

KEEP IT SIMPLE

Once the madeleines are cooled, dig out the core from the hump side. Fill with Speculoos ganache and replace the core.

Brush the whole madeleine with cinnamon glaze and allow to air-dry.

Melt the white chocolate and pipe over the bears to decorate as desired.

FEELING CONFIDENT? TRY THIS:

Once the madeleines are cooled, dig out the core from the front side. Fill with Speculoos ganache, as above.

CHOCOLATE SHELL Temper the Dulcey chocolate (page 42) and pour 15g (½oz) into each mould cavity.

Gently press the glazed madeleine into the mould and let it set at room temperature for at least 4 hours (or set at room temp for 1 hour and keep in the fridge for 10 mins – check carefully, as metal moulds in the fridge might cool down too fast and the chocolate shell might crack). Lightly cover the mould to prevent drying out.

Once fully set, carefully unmould.

Melt the white chocolate, pipe over the bears to decorate as desired.

MAKES

12

MOULD

Woojung / Chiyoda Madeleine 22mm (⅝in) deep

HOT CROSS MADELEINES

We wanted to capture everything we love about a hot cross bun in madeleine form. These are glazed with cinnamon, toasted, and finished with salted butter so the spices bloom and the butter melts in. Warm, sweet, and fragrant, they have all the comfort of the classic bun but with a lighter, tender crumb. Start night before.

INGREDIENTS

FRUIT MIX (SOAK 1 DAY AHEAD)

30g (1oz) raisins
30g (1oz) confit orange peel
equal quantities of Grand Marnier and spiced rum, just enough to submerge

HOT CROSS SPICE MIX (BY WEIGHT)

10g (2 tsp) ground cinnamon
5g (½tsp) part ground cloves
5g (½tsp) ground allspice

CINNAMON GLAZE

85g (3oz) icing (confectioners') sugar
25g (¾oz) water
pinch of ground cinnamon

HOT CROSS MADELEINE BATTER

120g (4½oz) cake flour
5g (½ tsp) baking powder
7g (¼oz) hot cross spice mix
3g (1 tsp) grated orange zest
pinch of sea salt
100g (3½oz) unsalted butter
7g (¼oz) milk
80g (2¾oz) whole eggs, strained (page 31)
75g (2⅔oz) caster sugar
10g (3 tsp) honey

CROSS ICING

150g (5¼oz) icing (confectioners') sugar
20g (1½oz) water

METHOD

TO SOAK THE FRUIT Combine the raisins and confit orange peel in a small container. Add a 1:1 ratio of Grand Marnier and spiced rum – just enough to submerge. Cover and soak overnight.

Drain the raisins well before use.

HOT CROSS SPICE MIX Mix together the cinnamon, cloves and allspice in the given proportions. Store in an airtight container.

CINNAMON GLAZE Sift the icing sugar and ground cinnamon into a bowl. Add the water and whisk until smooth. Set aside.

HOT CROSS MADELEINES Preheat the oven to 210°C fan (450°F/gas 9) and prepare your mould (page 29).

Sift the flour, baking powder, spices and salt, then set aside.

Melt the butter and milk together in a heatproof bowl over a pan of simmering water, keeping the temperature at 40°C (104°F).

Warm the eggs, sugar and honey to 30°C (86°F).

Mix the dry ingredients gently into the egg mixture, then mix in the butter one-third at a time.

Pipe into the moulds, then scatter the soaked fruit mix on top.

Reduce the oven temperature to 180°C (350°F/gas 4) and bake for 10 – 13 minutes until risen and set.

Remove from the oven, unmould and leave to cool slightly.

CROSS ICING Combine the icing sugar and water and whisk until smooth and pipeable. Transfer to a piping bag fitted with a flat nozzle. Cover half the nozzle with tape to create a thinner line.

IF YOU WANT TO ENJOY THEM FRESH:

Brush with cinnamon glaze. Let cool completely.

Pipe a cross over each madeleine using the prepared icing. Let the icing set at room temperature.

IF YOU WANT TO TOAST AND BUTTER THEM:

Skip the glazing part.

Slice the madeleines in half, toast lightly, and spread with butter for extra comfort.

MAKES

12 × 25g (¾oz) each,
or fill the mould by 80%

MOULD

Woojung Oval Financier

MADELEINE CELEBRATION TOWER

A Madeleine Tower is more than just a centerpiece. It is an experience meant for sharing, full of endless possibilities. You can create it in different colours, decorate it with ribbons or fresh flowers, and customise it to fit any occasion. Whether it is for a wedding, a birthday, or any special celebration, the tower becomes a showstopper. The delicate aroma of fresh pastries fills the air, and the tower's inviting shape brings everyone together.

At Madeleine de Proust, we customise our tower bases from SL Grade Polystyrene, carefully cutting them into neat, even tiers so each madeleine fits perfectly. In Australia, you can do the same with foam sourced from The Foam Company or other specialty suppliers. Every tower is festive, eye-catching, and always memorable, turning any milestone into something truly magical.

EACH LAYER DIMENSION

Circle 460mm (18in) diameter × 150mm (6in) thick
Circle 406mm (16in) diameter × 50mm (2in) thick
Circle 352mm (14in) diameter × 50mm (2in) thick
Circle 298mm (12in) diameter × 50mm (2in) thick
Circle 244mm (10in) diameter × 50mm (2in) thick
Circle 190mm (8in) diameter × 50mm (2in) thick
Circle 136mm (6in) diameter × 50mm (2in) thick
Circle 82mm (4in) diameter × 50mm (2in) thick

The widest is on the bottom.

MADELEINES NEEDED

around 150 pieces (tower size can be adjusted as needed)

METHOD

TO PREPARE THE TOWER STRUCTURE Cover each polystyrene layer with rolled fondant for a smooth, elegant finish.

Stick the fondant-covered layers together by inserting a toothpick through the centre of each circle to secure them. Alternatively, spray the entire tower with coloured cacao butter using a spray gun to match your theme or mood. Let the tower set completely before moving on.

SELECT YOUR MADELEINE SHAPE AND FLAVOUR Choose the madeleine design you want for the tower. For a consistent look, we tend to use silicone moulds.

During baking, gently place another silicone mould on top – this helps control the rise so the humps come out flatter, more even, and easier to assemble.

TO SET THE MADELEINES Prepare the madeleines as you like: fill them with custard, ganache, jam, or cream, coat them with chocolate, glaze lightly, or leave them natural for a rustic look.

Let the madeleines set completely before assembling to avoid smudging or sliding.

TO ATTACH THE MADELEINES TO THE TOWER Use melted chocolate as edible glue (a cooling spray helps set it instantly) or anchor with lollipop sticks/toothpicks – choose whichever suits your finish.

TO ASSEMBLE Begin at the top and work your way downwards (top to bottom), layer by layer.

Space the madeleines evenly, adjusting the angles slightly as you go to create a natural, flowing shape.

TO DECORATE After assembling, weave in fresh flowers, herbs, berries, or seasonal accents between the madeleines to add romance, colour or celebration to your final tower.

MAKES

12

MOULD

Woojung Oval Financier

PINK CARNATION MADELEINES

Just three months after we opened Madeleine de Proust, I lost my mum. Without her presence, everything felt incredibly difficult. I kept thinking about all the things I still wanted to say, and all the little ways I wished I could care for her again. Out of those feelings, I created this madeleine. Pink for love, and for cancer awareness. It is soft and floral, with delicate notes that feel like a quiet embrace. This piece carries my heart, and I hope it brings comfort to anyone who has ever missed someone deeply, especially on days that are meant to be shared.

INGREDIENTS

YUZU SYRUP
25g caster (superfine) sugar
25g (1¾oz) yuzu juice

YUZU GLAZE
85g (3oz) icing (confectioners') sugar
25g (¾oz) yuzu juice

LEMON YUZU GANACHE
100g (20oz) double (heavy) cream
30g (1oz) glucose syrup
130g (4¼oz) white chocolate
20g (4 tsp) lemon juice
30g (1oz) unsalted butter
10g (2 tsp) yuzu juice
3g (1 tsp) citric acid

BLACK TEA GANACHE
150g (5¼oz) double (heavy) cream
15g (½oz) honey
3g (¼ tsp) Assam tea leaves
150g (5¼oz) white chocolate
5g (1 tsp) unsalted butter

PINK CHOCOLATE ENROBAGE
200g (7oz) white chocolate
100g (3¼oz) cocoa butter
small pinch of pink fat-soluble food colouring
small pinch of purple fat-soluble food colouring

MADELEINE BATTER
95g (3¼oz) cake flour
5g (1 tsp) baking powder
pinch of sea salt
75g (2½oz) unsalted butter
5g (1 tsp) milk
60g (2oz) whole eggs, strained (page 31)
60g (2oz) caster (superfine) sugar
7g (¼ tsp) honey
3g (1 tsp) lemon zest

FOR DECORATION
chocolate crunchy pearls (dusted with rose gold powder)

METHOD

YUZU SYRUP Combine the sugar and yuzu juice in a pan and bring to the boil. Remove from heat and let cool completely before use.

YUZU GLAZE Sift the icing sugar into a bowl. Add the yuzu juice and whisk until smooth. Set aside for use just before assembling.

LEMON YUZU GANACHE Heat the cream and glucose syrup until warm. Pour over the white chocolate and emulsify with a spatula. Mix in the lemon juice, yuzu juice, butter, and citric acid until smooth. Cover with clingfilm (plastic wrap) and refrigerate until set.

BLACK TEA GANACHE Heat the cream and honey together and infuse with Assam tea for 5 minutes. Strain to remove the leaves. Pour over the white chocolate and blend to emulsify. Add the butter and mix until smooth. Chill until slightly firm, then whip together with buttercream until fluffy.

PINK CHOCOLATE ENROBAGE Melt white chocolate and cocoa butter to 40°C (104°F). Add the pink and purple colouring powders and blend well.

MADELEINES Preheat the oven to 210°C fan (450°F/gas 9) and prepare your mould (page 29).

Sift the flour, baking powder and salt, then set aside.

Melt the butter and milk together in a heatproof bowl over a pan of simmering water, keeping the temperature at 40°C (104°F).

Warm the eggs, sugar, honey and lemon zest to 30°C (86°F).

Mix the dry ingredients gently into the egg mixture, then mix in the butter one-third at a time.

Pipe into the moulds, reduce the oven temperature to 180°C (350°F/gas 4) and bake for 10 – 13 minutes until risen and set.

Remove from the oven, unmould, and leave to cool slightly.

TO FINISH Brush the madeleines with yuzu syrup while still warm. Let cool completely.

Glaze the hump or belly side with the yuzu glaze, let it dry.

Dig out the core from the flat side and fill with lemon yuzu ganache.

Pipe black tea ganache on the surface using a Loyal Petal No.125 nozzle to form a carnation. Freeze until fully set.

Prepare the pink chocolate enrobage and dip the frozen madeleines using a small offset spatula.

Decorate with rose gold – dusted crunchy pearls. Leave to set before serving.

NOTE

This recipe is a little more technical, but it's incredibly rewarding if you're up for a fun baking challenge.

POPPIN' CORN MADELEINES

We never expected this one to take off on social media. Poppin' Corn was inspired by the sweetcorn sandwich ice cream you find in Korea – playful, creamy and nostalgic. It took months to get the look and flavour just right. Each kernel is piped by hand, finished with chocolate leaves and kadaif for corn silk. The result is a madeleine that is as much fun to eat as it is to look at, with a sweet, buttery taste and a gentle pop from the sweet corn in every bite.

INGREDIENTS

POPCORN GANACHE
25g (¾oz) popped corn
100g (3¼oz) double (heavy) cream
75g (2½oz) milk
7g (¼oz) glucose syrup
85g (3oz) corn chocolate (we use Ecuador from Republica del Cacao) or caramelized white chocolate
10g (⅓oz) cocoa butter

POPCORN PIPING CREAM
100g (3¼oz) popcorn ganache
200g (7oz) Swiss buttercream (page 46)

COOKED CORN FILLING
80g (2¾oz) drained canned unsweetened, unsalted corn kernels
15g (½oz) caster (superfine) sugar
pinch of sea salt

CREAM CHEESE BUTTERCREAM
80g (2¾oz) cream cheese
80g (2¾oz) Swiss buttercream (page 46)

BROWN BUTTER MADELEINE BATTER
125g (4½oz) cake flour
5g (1 tsp) baking powder
3g (1 tsp) caramelized milk powder (page 47)
pinch of sea salt
105g (3½oz) butter
7g (1¼oz) milk
85g (3oz) whole eggs, strained (page 31)
80g (2¾oz) caster (superfine) sugar
10g (⅓oz) Leatherwood honey

FINAL CORN FILLING MIXTURE
80g (2¾oz) cooked corn
160g (5½oz) cream cheese buttercream

YELLOW CHOCOLATE SPRAY
150g (5½oz) white chocolate
5g (¾ tsp) titanium dioxide
5g (¾ tsp) yellow fat-soluble colouring
200g (7oz) cocoa butter

GREEN CHOCOLATE LEAF
400g (14oz) corn chocolate (I use Republica del Cacao)
2g (½ tsp) yellow fat-soluble food colouring
1.7g (¼ tsp) green fat-soluble food colouring

EDIBLE CORN SILK
50g (1¾oz) dark chocolate
7g (1 tsp) cocoa (unsweetened chocolate) powder (Dutch-processed)
80g (2¾oz) kadaif, toasted
pinch of sea salt

NOTE

This recipe is a little more technical, but it's incredibly rewarding if you're up for a fun baking challenge.

METHOD

POPCORN GANACHE Warm the cream and milk, then pour over the popped corn. Blend finely, then strain.

Reheat the liquid to 80°C (175°F). Pour over the corn chocolate and cocoa butter, then emulsify with a hand blender. Let crystallize overnight in the fridge.

POPCORN PIPING CREAM Whip the popcorn ganache and buttercream until fluffy. Transfer to a piping bag fitted with a No.6 round tip.

COOKED CORN FILLING Combine the drained corn, sugar and salt in a pan. Cook until the liquid evaporates completely. Let cool.

CREAM CHEESE BUTTERCREAM Mix the cream cheese and buttercream until fluffy and smooth. Combine with cooked corn to create the final corn filling.

MADELEINES Preheat the oven to 210°C fan (450°F/gas 9) and prepare your mould (page 29).

Sift the flour, caramelized milk powder, baking powder and salt, then set aside.

Melt the butter and milk together in a heatproof bowl over a pan of simmering water, keeping the temperature at 40°C (104°F).

Warm the eggs, sugar and honey to 30°C (86°F).

Mix the dry ingredients gently into the egg mixture, then mix in the butter one-third at a time.

Pipe into the moulds, reduce the oven temperature to 180°C (350°F/gas 4) and bake for 10 – 13 minutes until risen and set.

Remove from the oven, unmould and leave to cool. Once baked, let cool and dig out the core from the front. Fill with the corn cream cheese mixture.

TO DECORATE Pipe corn kernels using popcorn piping cream. Freeze until set.

YELLOW CHOCOLATE SPRAY Prepare and temper to 32°C (page 42). Spray over the front of the frozen madeleines. Keep frozen.

GREEN CHOCOLATE LEAF Cut a teflon sheet into leaf shapes. Temper the green-coloured corn chocolate and spread onto the sheet.

Attach to the side of the madeleine. After 5 minutes, remove the sheet.

Use more green chocolate to connect the base and leaf. Add texture with an offset spatula.

EDIBLE CORN SILK Mix the dark chocolate, cocoa powder, kadaif and salt. Form strands and attach to the top to finish.

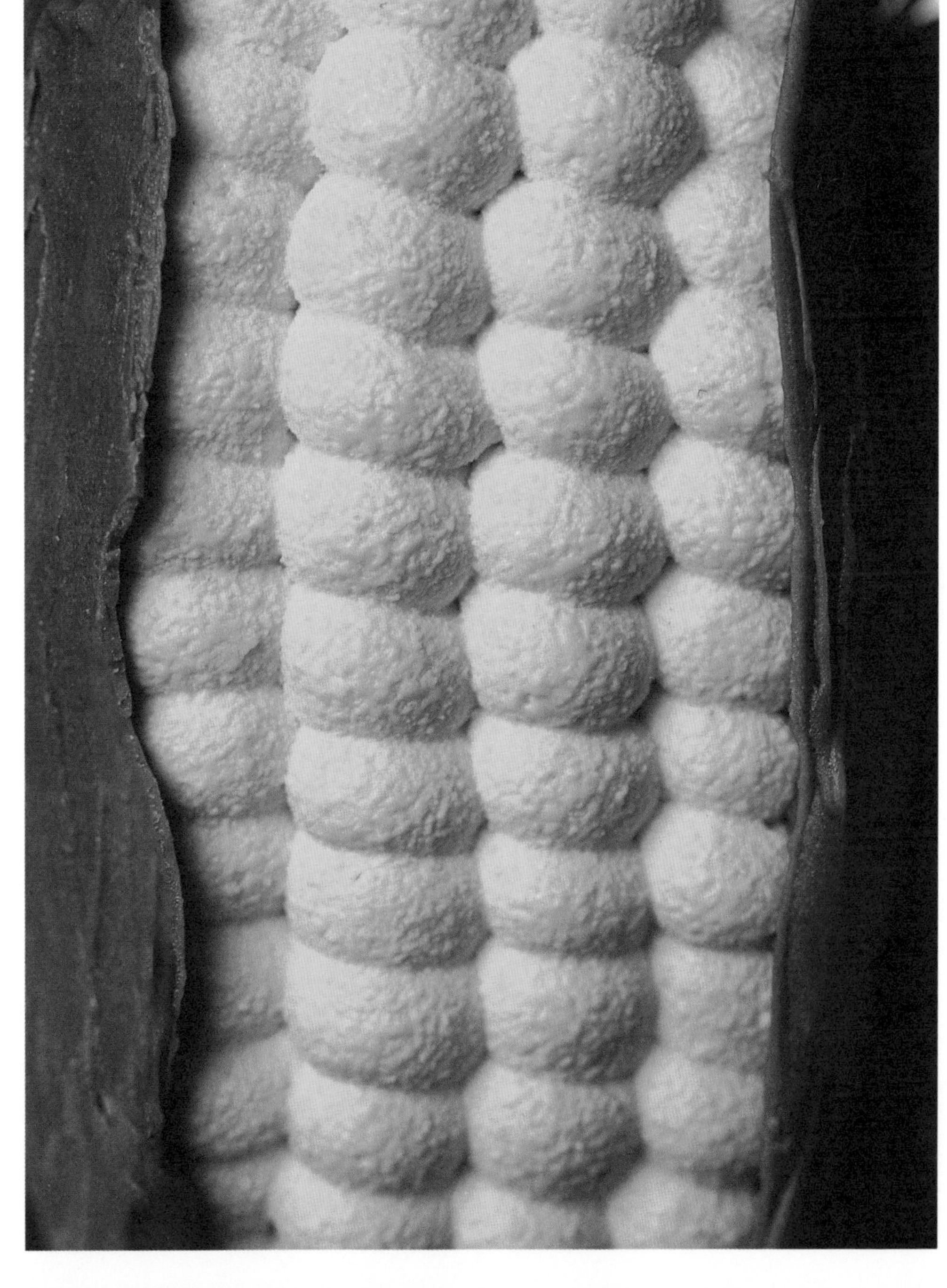

Savoury madeleines aren't something you see every day – and to be honest, we don't make them all that often either. There are plenty of wild combinations out there, but I prefer to keep things gentle and fun. We love playing with both sweet and savoury together, rather than going fully savoury – what we call 'dan-jjan dan-jjan' in Korean, that addictive sweet-salty mix. These two recipes are our own playful take: madeleines cleverly disguised as onigiri and truffles, but with that signature soft texture and creamy filling inside.

SAVOURY

MAKES

24

MOULD

Truffle mould from Mold Brother

BLACK TRUFFLE MADELEINES

Created for a collaboration with NOMAD Melbourne, this madeleine is a playful tribute to truffle season – a treat that looks just like a truffle, but hides a surprise inside. The soft, buttery sponge is filled with rich truffle cheesecake cream, bringing earthy depth and creamy tang to every bite. Elegant on the outside, luscious and unexpected within, it's a celebration of flavour, fun, and a memorable collaboration.

INGREDIENTS

TRUFFLE CHEESECAKE CREAM

75g (2½oz) cream cheese
75g (2½oz) mascarpone
12g (½oz) light brown sugar
45g (1½oz) sugar
20g (⅔oz) whole egg
5g (¾ tsp) egg yolk
7g (1 tsp) corn starch
65g (2¼oz) whipping cream
7g (1 tsp) black truffle paste

TRUFFLE MADELEINE BATTER

125g (4½oz)cake flour
5g (¾ tsp) baking powder
3g (½ tsp) caramelised milk powder
105g (3½oz) unsalted butter
7g (1 tsp) milk
85g (3oz) whole egg
80g (2¾) caster sugar
10g (½ tsp) honey
3g (½ tsp) black truffle paste
pinch of sea salt

BLACK CHOCOLATE ENROBAGE

200g (7oz) dark chocolate
200g (7oz) cocoa butter

BLACK CHOCOLATE SPRAY

200g (7oz) dark chocolate
400g (14oz) cocoa butter
7g (1 tsp) black oil-based food colouring
4g (⅔ tsp) black oil-based food colouring

TIP

If you don't blend the cheesecake mix after baking, you can chill and enjoy it as a truffle cheesecake instead.

METHOD

TRUFFLE CHEESECAKE CREAM Preheat the oven to 180°C (fan). Soften the cream cheese in the microwave (just to room temperature, not melted). In a stand mixer fitted with the paddle attachment, combine the cream cheese, light brown sugar, and sugar. Mix on low speed for about 5 minutes, until the sugar is fully incorporated.

Sift in the corn starch and mix until no powder remains. Add the eggs and egg yolk, mixing well until fully combined. Add the mascarpone and mix gently. Add the double cream and mix until smooth.

Pour the mixture into a small pan or baking tray and bake for 25 minutes, or until the top is caramelised and the internal temperature reaches 83°C. Remove from the oven and transfer to a food processor. Blend on high speed until smooth. Transfer to a piping bag and chill in the fridge until ready to use.

TRUFFLE MADELEINE Preheat the oven to 210°C fan (450°F/gas 9).

Sift the flour, baking powder, caramelized milk powder, and salt, then set aside.

Melt the butter and milk together in a heatproof bowl over a pan of simmering water, keeping the temperature at 40°C (104°F).

Warm the eggs, sugar and honey to 30°C (86°F).

Mix the dry ingredients gently into the egg mixture, then mix in the butter one-third at a time.

Pipe into the moulds, reduce the oven temperature to 180°C (350°F/gas 4) and bake for 15 minutes, until risen and set.

Remove from the oven, unmould and leave to cool for at least 30 minutes.

Core the back of each madeleine and fill with truffle cheesecake cream. Replace the removed core (page 38). Freeze them at least 4 hours.

AT THIS POINT, YOU CAN FINISH YOUR MADELEINES IN TWO WAYS:

KEEP IT SIMPLE

Melt the dark chocolate, cocoa butter and colouring together until smooth (keep at 35°C for dipping).

Dip the frozen truffle madeleines into the chocolate enrobage, let excess drip off, and set on a tray lined with baking paper.

Let set in the fridge before serving.

FEELING CONFIDENT? TRY THIS:

Melt the dark chocolate, cocoa butter and black oil-based colouring together until fully emulsified. Keep at 35°C for spraying.

Spray the frozen truffle madeleines with the black chocolate spray using a spray gun. Let set in the fridge before serving.

MAKES

8

MOULD

Triangle Silicone

CHEESE ONIGIRI MADELEINES

Inspired by onigiri – *samgak kimbap* in Korea – this madeleine is a playful twist on a classic shape. The tender, golden sponge is moulded to look just like an onigiri and filled with a silky Comté miso custard. The first taste is soft and savoury, with a gentle sweetness and deep umami from the custard filling. It's a little savoury comfort, wrapped up in something new.

INGREDIENTS

COMTÉ MISO CUSTARD

175g (6oz) double (heavy) cream
115g (8oz) whole milk
30g (3¼oz) milk powder
10g white miso
75g (5¼oz) egg yolks
30g (1oz) Comté, finely grated

NORI PARMESAN MADELEINE BATTER

115g (4oz) cake flour
5g (¼oz) baking powder
3g (pinch) sea salt
115g (4oz) whole eggs, strained (page 31)
30g (1oz) caster (superfine) sugar
10g (⅓oz) honey
85g (3oz) olive oil
5g (1 tsp) coarsely crushed seasoned seaweed
35g ((¼oz) Parmesan cheese, finely grated

GARNISH

caster sugar, for brûlée
1 sheet of nori, cut into small rectangles

METHOD

COMTÉ MISO CUSTARD In a saucepan, combine the cream, milk, milk powder and white miso. Bring to a boil.

Pour the hot infused liquid over the egg yolks and whisk until fully combined. Transfer to a baking dish and bake, uncovered, at 180°C (350°F) for 30 minutes, until the top is caramelized and the internal temperature is over 83°C. Scoop out and blend in a food processor until smooth.

Cool to 40°C (104°F), add the grated Comté (season to taste) and blend again until fully emulsified. Chill and transfer to a piping bag.

NORI PARMESAN MADELEINE Preheat the oven to 210°C fan (450°F/gas 9) and prepare your mould (page 29).

Sift the flour, baking powder and salt, then set aside.

Warm the eggs, sugar and honey to 30°C (86°F).

Add the dry ingredients and mix gently until combined. Stir in the olive oil, followed by the seaweed and Parmesan until evenly distributed.

Spray a triangular silicone mould with oil and pipe the batter 70% full. Place a Silpat and metal tray on top of the mould. Bake at 180°C fan (400°F/gas 6) for 14 – 15 minutes until golden.

Remove from the oven and leave to cool. You can pop the madeleines out once it's cooled.

TO ASSEMBLE & GARNISH Slightly brush the outer layer with water and cover with caster sugar.

Use an apple corer to create a cavity from the bottom part (the part you will cover with the nori). Pipe the Comté miso custard into the centre of each madeleine and replace the core.

Slightly brush the outer layer again with water and cover with caster sugar, then use a blow torch to brûlée.

Wrap the base with a small rectangle of nori, like an onigiri.

BRANDS & SUPPLIERS

Here are some of the brands we prefer to use, along with international suppliers of the best-quality equipment and ingredients. Check your local sources, as availability may differ by region.

INGREDIENTS

CHOCOLATE

Valrhona and Republica del Cacao

AUSTRALIA Retail at Simon Johnson; wholesale via Calendar Cheese.

FLOUR

Nisshin Violet flour

AUSTRALIA Available at Japanese grocers such as FUJI Mart (Melbourne).

Gluten-free plain flour from White Wings (available at Woolworths).

HONEY

We use Backyard Honey and The Tasmanian Honey Company.

CEREMONIAL MATCHA POWDER

We source our matcha through Hello Matcha. hello-matcha.com.au

VANILLA

Norohy

AUSTRALIA Wholesale via Calendar Cheese. Or Heilala (available at Woolworths).

FRUIT PURÉES

Adamance – Exceptional fruit purées made from carefully selected fruit, with no added sugar.

AUSTRALIA Wholesale via Calendar Cheese.

Boiron – High-quality fruit purées.

AUSTRALIA Wholesale via Eustralis Food.

CREAM

We use Elle & Vire and Anchor.

AUSTRALIA Wholesale via Eustralis Food.

COCONUT CREAM

We use Kara.

BUTTER

We use Anchor or Lescure French butter (occasionally found at Coles). For everyday use in Australia, Western Star (found at Woolworths or Coles) is a good alternative.

FAT-SOLUBLE COLOURING

Roberts Edible Craft
ediblecraft.com.au

OTHER INGREDIENTS

SUGARS, BAKING POWDER AND OTHER BASICS

We use standard supermarket brands.

NUTS AND NUT PASTES

We prefer freshly roasted nuts and 100% nut pastes from reputable grocers or specialty shops.

MOULDS & EQUIPMENT

MOULDS

Here are some of the moulds we use most often:

MADELEINE/LEMON MOULD Woojung – Available to order through our website – madeleinedeproust.com.au

MADELEINE/CACAO/BANANA MOULD: Chiyoda – Sourced from Japan (the shop is called Majimaya in Tokyo – we usually ask friends to bring these back).

TRUFFLE MOULD: Mold Brothers.

TRIANGLE SILICONE MOULD: Martellato.

BEAR (KUMAGORO) MOULD: Matsunaga.

For silicone moulds, most can be easily found by searching online or at specialty baking shops.

FOAM FOR MADELEINE TOWER

We get it custom-made from The Foam Company.

ACKNOWLEDGEMENTS

What started as a small, nostalgic idea grew into something real because of the kindness, effort and support of so many people around us.

FROM US

To ZK, Yungting, Shanelle, and Sophy – our very first team. You were there when it was just us, folding boxes, piping batter, and building something from scratch with heart and hustle.

To our early believers – Tara, Hani, Ed, Mo, Emma, Dennis, and more – thank you for cheering us on, believing in us, and coming to see us every day, every week. You gave us the courage to keep going.

To our team at Madeleine de Proust – past and present – thank you for showing up every day with care, pride and humour. We are only as good as the people beside us.

To everyone who visits us – you welcomed our madeleines into your most personal moments. You gave our work meaning, again and again.

To our Melbourne 'family' – Biggie, Sunny, Pearl, Leo, and Aadi – thank you for being around us, supporting us, and making this city feel like home.

To the incredible team behind this book:

Eve, for believing in our story and giving us the opportunity to share what we do. You wouldn't believe the feeling we had when we received the first email from you – it still feels surreal.

Michael, our friend and photographer – thank you for capturing the soul of each madeleine with such generosity.

Evi, for designing pages that truly bring our vision to life.

Lee, for your thoughtful styling and the care you brought to every detail.

To the team at Quadrille – thank you for embracing our small cakes and helping us share its story with the world.

FROM JU

First and foremost, my deepest thanks go to Rong – for always being by my side as a partner and friend, and for your unwavering support. Everything we've achieved was only possible because we did it together.

To my mother – thank you for always believing in me, and for reminding me that I could do anything I set my heart on.

To my father – my shelter, my teacher in dedication. Through your life, you showed me what it means to work with purpose and heart. Thank you for being my foundation.

To my sister, my brother, Eunji, and Yujin – thank you for loving me unconditionally, for supporting my dreams without ever asking why. Your love gave me the courage to keep going.

Without you all, this journey would not have been possible. Thank you – and I love you.

FROM RONG

To Ju – for your steadiness, your faith, and the way you bring quiet magic to everything. You make the impossible possible and bring our dream to life. Thank you for being in my corner, always.

To my mom and dad – thank you for your unconditional support, for your understanding, and for letting me chase impossible ideas without ever asking me to play it safe. I owe you both so much.

To my brothers – thank you for being supportive and for always offering feedback and ideas.

To my friends – for your encouragement and for always being there to try our madeleines, no matter how many experiments it took.

ABOUT THE AUTHORS

HYOJU PARK

Hyoju began her pastry journey in South Korea, where a childhood fascination with baking turned into a lifelong pursuit. She went on to train in London and returned to Seoul to work at Mingles, later becoming head pastry chef at Attica in Melbourne. Known for her quiet precision and thoughtful approach, Ju brings a sense of calm, detail and depth to everything she creates.

RONG YAO SOH

Rong's path began in London's Michelin-starred kitchens before bringing him to Melbourne's vibrant culinary scene. He is driven by curiosity, creativity and a love for stories – especially the ones you can taste. His work blends nostalgia, boldness and a refusal to do things the ordinary way.

Together, they are the co-founders of Madeleine de Proust.

MADELEINE
MADELEINE

Quadrille, Penguin Random House UK,
One Embassy Gardens, 8 Viaduct Gardens,
London SW11 7BW

Quadrille Publishing Limited is part of the Penguin Random House group of companies whose addresses can be found at global.penguinrandomhouse.com

Published by Quadrille in 2026

www.penguin.co.uk

A CIP catalogue record for this book is available from the British Library

ISBN 978-1-83783-491-4
10 9 8 7 6 5 4 3 2 1

Managing Director, Publishing: Sarah Lavelle
Editorial Director: Sophie Allen
Senior Commissioning Editor: Eve Marleau
Editor: Phoebe Bath
Design: Evi.O-Studio
Photographer: Michael Gardenia
Food and Prop Stylist: Lee Blaylock
Senior Production Controller: Martina Georgieva

Colour reproduction by F1

Printed in China by C&C Offset Printing Co., Ltd.

The authorized representative in the EEA is Penguin Random House Ireland, Morrison Chambers, 32 Nassau Street, Dublin D02 YH68.

Penguin Random House is committed to a sustainable future for our business, our readers and our planet. This book is made from Forest Stewardship Council® certified paper.